The
University of
Chicago
School
Mathematics
Project

TRANSITION MATHEMATICS

ASSESSMENT RESOURCES
VOLUME 1 • CHAPTERS 1-6

About Assessment
Assessment Forms
Chapter Quizzes
Chapter Tests, Forms A, B, C, and D
Chapter Tests, Cumulative Form
Comprehensive Tests
Answers
Evaluation Guides

Mc Graw Hill **Wright Group**

The **McGraw-Hill** Companies

www.WrightGroup.com

 **Wright Group**

Copyright © 2008 by Wright Group/McGraw-Hill.

Printed in the United States of America.

Send all inquiries to:
Wright Group/McGraw-Hill
P.O. Box 812960
Chicago, IL 60681

ISBN 978-0-07-618586-3
MHID 0-07-618586-9

2 3 4 5 6 7 8 9 VHG 13 12 11 10 09 08 07

The *McGraw-Hill* Companies

Contents

Volume 1

The Changing Face of Mathematics Instruction and Assessment

The National Council of Teachers of Mathematics and other mathematics education organizations have recommended that teachers use diverse methods of instruction in order to address varied learning styles of students. Such methods include activities, open-ended investigations, long-term projects, and the use of cooperative learning.

Instruction and assessment are closely linked. As teachers use diverse instructional methods, they also need to consider diverse methods of assessment and evaluation. According to the NCTM Assessment Standards, *assessment* is defined as the process of gathering evidence about a student's knowledge of, ability to use, and disposition toward, mathematics and of making inferences from that evidence for a variety of purposes. *Evaluation* is the process of determining the worth of, or assigning a value to, something on the basis of careful examination and judgment. Effective methods of assessment offer students opportunities to demonstrate how they approach problem situations, collect and organize information, formulate and test conjectures, and communicate their mathematical insights.

A good assessment program contains tasks that are appropriate to the topics students are learning and provide outcomes valuable to students. Such an assessment program allows for individual factors as a school's curriculum objectives, a teacher's style of instruction, and a student's maturity level and preferred learning style. Each individual teacher determines an assessment program that best suits the needs of his or her students.

> When teachers are selecting assessment methods, the age, experience, and special needs of students should be considered. Teachers must ensure that all students have an opportunity to demonstrate clearly and completely what they know and what they can do.
>
> *Principles and Standards for School Mathematics*

Materials Provided in *Assessment Resources*

To help a teacher select the most appropriate assessment and/or evaluation tools for his or her classroom, this resource provides the following materials.

Assessment Forms

- student-completed forms
- teacher-completed forms for individual, group, and class activities

Assessment Instruments

- **Chapter Quizzes,** two per chapter, which cover three or four lessons and which contain mostly constructed-response items
- **Chapter Tests, Forms A and B,** which are alternate versions of each other and which assess every chapter objective in primarily constructed-response format
- **Chapter Tests, Form C,** which consist of 4 to 6 performance-based, open-ended items, many of which assess several chapter objectives simultaneously
- **Chapter Tests, Form D,** which are performance based and which often assess 5 or more chapter objectives as applied to a single task
- **Chapter Tests, Cumulative Form,** which contain mostly constructed-response items
- **Comprehensive Tests,** every three or four chapters, which are cumulative in nature and consist primarily of multiple-choice items

State Tests and the No Child Left Behind Act

Given the requirements of the No Child Left Behind Act and high-stakes state tests, it is important that students have experiences with the types of items found on state tests. Many state tests include multiple-choice items. The multiple-choice items throughout the text and on the test forms give students experience with this type of assessment. If your state's assessment includes performance tasks, then you may want to assign items from the Form C or D test on a regular basis. As indicated in the section on writing, we would suggest that you score such performance tasks using the rubric applied in your state.

In addition to formal assessments, such as tests and quizzes, teachers should be continually gathering information about their students' progress through informal means, such as asking questions during the course of a lesson, conducting interviews with individual students, and giving writing prompts.

Principles and Standards for School Mathematics

Guidelines for Developing an Effective Assessment Program

Developing an effective program of assessment is an ongoing process. Some assessment instruments will seem perfectly suited to the teacher and his or her students from the start. Others may be effective only after the teacher has had a chance to experiment and refine them. Still others may be inappropriate for a given class or instructional situation. The following are some guidelines that may be helpful when choosing the types of assessment for a particular program.

Assessment serves many purposes.

- For the teacher, assessment yields feedback on the appropriateness of instructional methods and offers some clues as to how the content or pace of instruction could be modified.
- For students, assessment identifies areas for improvement and affirms their successes.
- Sometimes, assessments evaluate student performance to assign a grade.

The assessment process should be a positive experience for students.

- Teachers should use a variety of assessment techniques.
- Assessment provides opportunities for students to demonstrate their mathematical capabilities in an atmosphere that encourages maximum performance.
- Assessment should emphasize what students *do* know and *can* do, not just what they do not know and cannot do.
- Teachers motivate students to achieve by using tasks that reflect the value of students' efforts.

Good assessments address higher-order thinking skills.

- Teachers should design assessments that provide a picture of the student as a critical thinker and problem solver.
- Teachers should use assessments that identify *how* the student does mathematics, not just what answer he or she gets.

Assessment activities should resemble day-to-day tasks.

- Assessment activities should be similar to instructional activities.
- Assessment activities should further instruction.
- Students should receive immediate and detailed feedback in order to further the learning process.
- Teachers should encourage students to explore how the mathematics they are learning applies to real situations.

Students should be encouraged to engage in self-assessment.

- Students should reflect on what they have done.
- Students should share their goals for assessment.

Portfolios and Notebooks

A *portfolio* is a collection of a student's work—projects, reports, drawings, reflections, representative assignments, assessment instruments—that displays the student's mathematical accomplishments over an extended period. *The following suggestions for use should be adapted to the needs and organizational style of each situation.*

A *student notebook* reflects a student's day-to-day activities related to the mathematics class. It may include a section for journal entries as well as sections for homework, tests, and notes.

Getting Started
- Provide file folders labeled *Portfolio*.
- Provide guidelines for notebook format.

A Portfolio
- A portfolio can be used as the basis for assessing a student's achievements. The focus of the portfolio should be on student thinking, growth in understanding over time, making mathematical connections, positive attitudes about mathematics, and the problem-solving process.
- The teacher also selects student materials for the portfolio and includes any appropriate assessment instruments.
- The student completes the *About My Portfolio* form.
- Portfolios may include student selected items from the notebook; a letter from the student describing the work; a math autobiography; other work selected by the teacher including math surveys; various assessment documents.

A Notebook
- A notebook is for "work in progress." The student should keep in it all class and reading notes, group work, homework, reports and projects, and various student assessment forms, such as *Student Self-Assessment*.
- Every two to six weeks, students review their notebooks to determine the materials they would like to transfer to their portfolios.

> [Portfolios] involve students in a "draft and revise" approach to doing mathematical work and model how mathematics work is often done outside school.
>
> *Mathematics Assessment: A Practical Handbook for Grades 6-8 (NCTM Publication)*

Evaluating a Portfolio
- Teachers and students should keep in mind that portfolio evaluation is a matter of ongoing discussion.
- Teachers should set aside time to discuss the portfolio with the student.
- Teachers might use the portfolio when discussing the student's progress with his or her family.
- Teachers and students might use a portfolio as a basis for identifying strengths and weaknesses and for setting goals for the next block of work.
- Teachers should consider developing their own criteria for evaluating portfolios, such as numeric scales, based on the needs of their students.

Evaluating a Notebook
- Notebooks should be evaluated based on agreed-upon guidelines.
- Notebooks should be evaluated for organization and neatness, completeness, and timeliness.
- Notebooks may be evaluated by checking items or by assigning numeric values to specific items.
- Notebooks should be evaluated on a regular basis as determined by the teacher (e.g., every week or every chapter).

Using Free-Response and Multiple-Choice Tests

Teachers use written tests for many purposes. Particularly when it is objective-referenced, a test can be a relatively quick and efficient method of diagnosing the scope of a student's mathematical knowledge. Tests can also provide valuable instructional feedback. And, of course, grades are a traditional instrument for reporting student achievement to parents, administrators, and the community. This book provides a large number of both constructed-response and multiple-choice items.

Constructed-Response Tests

A constructed-response test is a collection of items for which a student must supply requested information. Although constructed-response tests are generally designed for written responses, they may also be used orally with individual students, especially those with limited English proficiency.

Multiple-Choice Tests

A multiple-choice test consists of many well-defined problems or questions. The student is given a set of four or five possible answers for each item and is asked to select the correct or best answer. The other choices, often called distractors, usually reflect common misconceptions or errors.

Assessment Resources contains:
- Quizzes covering three or four lessons in each chapter. The quizzes are primarily constructed-response in nature.
- Chapter Tests, Forms A and B, which are alternate forms of each other and which test every chapter objective. The tests contain primarily constructed-response items, but they may also include several multiple-choice items. These tests can be used as chapter pretests and posttests to help implement needed individualized instruction.
- Chapter Tests, Cumulative Form, for Chapters 2–12, which are basically constructed-response assessment. About half of the tests' content comes from previous chapters.
- Comprehensive Tests for Chapters 1–3, 1–6, 1–9, and 1–12, which consist of mostly multiple-choice items. These tests can be used primarily as quarter, semester, or end-of-year assessments. Test items are evenly divided among chapters covered.

Using Technology on Assessments

If students use calculators and other technology as part of instruction, then they should be allowed to use that technology on assessments. Otherwise, instruction and assessment are not aligned. If there are some computations and procedures you want your students to be able to do without technology (for example, basic computations with integers), you might have a portion of an assessment on which calculators are not permitted. You might reproduce this portion on colored paper. When students complete this portion and turn it in, they can obtain the remainder of the test and use the calculator to complete it. The use of calculators is assumed on all the quizzes and tests contained in this book.

Students may need guidance about what to record on their paper when they use technology to solve a problem. You might have them write the key sequence they use or write a formula or equation and show what values they substituted. If they have graphed an equation, have them indicate the window (the minimum and maximum values for x and y) and several key points. Many students have difficulty transferring graphs from their calculator to paper and may need guidance in this regard. Some teachers have students print out their calculator screens if the equipment is available.

At times, you might ask students to create a calculator graph as part of an in-class assessment. You can circulate around the room to check their work. If students need to input a long set of data as part of an assessment, you can save class time by asking them to enter the data at home. The next day, you can check that they have entered the values correctly. Data can also be quickly entered by linking one student's calculator to another.

Using Performance Assessment

Performance assessments allow students to apply their knowledge to a particular task. They are designed to reveal how a student approaches a problem, reasons through its solution, and defends the result. A good performance task can be approached in many different ways and may even have more than one acceptable solution.

Using a General Rubric

Rubrics are a useful tool for evaluating student work on a performance assessment. Rubrics are not the same as partial credit. With partial credit, a teacher assigns different numbers of points to different items based on the work students complete. By contrast, rubrics are assigned on a conceptual basis so that a particular score is consistent across all tasks. The general rubric below can be used to score a wide range of constructed response items.

Successful responses

4 The solution is complete and accurate. The solution is essentially a model solution.

3 The solution is almost complete and accurate. There may be some minor errors in notation or computation that are clerical, rather than conceptual, in nature.

Unsuccessful responses

2 The solution is in the proper direction and has substance. The solution may stop about halfway, although there is a chain of reasoning. Or, the solution contains a major conceptual error.

1 The solution indicates some appropriate entry into the problem but a major impasse is reached early. There is no chain of reasoning.

0 The work is wrong or mathematically meaningless. There is no correct mathematics embedded in the solution.

Although specific rubrics might be written for each item to indicate expected responses that would generate scores from 0 through 4, a general rubric is still needed for unusual or unexpected responses.

A benefit of using rubrics is that a score of 2 has the same meaning across multiple items. This can be helpful when diagnosing performance. For instance, suppose five items are scored using the above rubric. One student has scores of 2, 2, 2, 2, and 2; a second student has scores of 4, 0, 4, 0, and 2. Both students have an overall score of 10, but their performance is quite different. The first student gets about halfway on all five items. The second student really knows the content of two items, gets about halfway on a third item, and can make no progress at all on two of the items. Different instructional approaches might be needed to help these two students improve their understanding.

Caution: Rubrics should not be converted to grades in terms of percentages. A score of 3 is a successful response, and should not be assigned a grade of 75%. Grades might be assigned as 4 (A), 3 (B), 2 (C), 1 (D), and 0 (F) or as 4 (A), 3 (A-), 2 (B- or C+), 1 (C or C-), and 1 (D) (Thompson and Senk 1998).

Chapter Tests, Form C

The Form C Chapter Tests provided in this resource help you make a judgment of your students' understanding of mathematical concepts and their ability to interpret information, make generalizations, and communicate their ideas. Each assessment contains four to six open-ended questions, each of which is keyed to several chapter objectives.

Administering Form C Tests

The tests can be administered in a way that is best suited for your students. Provide manipulatives, extra paper, and other tools as needed. The use of calculators is assumed.

- Use all the assessment items.
- Use only one or two, along with a constructed-response or a multiple-choice test.
- Use the assessment items to interview each student.
- Have students give the explanations orally, and then write the answers.

Evaluating Form C Tests

Each test item is accompanied by a list of two or more evaluation criteria that can be used as a basis for judging student responses.

+	excellent
✓	satisfactory
–	inadequate

To rate how well students meet each criterion, a simple scale such as this may be used.

	Form C Tests	Constructed-Response Tests
Number of Items	4–6	15–35
Sample Item	• Draw 3 different rectangles that each have an area of 12 square centimeters.	• Find the area of a rectangle that is 4 centimeters long and 3 centimeters wide.
Mode of Administration	• Interview • Written Response • Combination of interview and written response	• Written response
Answers	• May have more than one • May require an explanation by student	• Usually single, short
Scoring	• 2–4 evaluation criteria • Use of simple rating scale • Rubrics applied to score individual items	• One correct answer for each item
Benefits	• More accurate determination of instructional needs and strengths of students	• Similar to the Self-Test and Chapter (SPUR) Review in the Student Edition, easy to score

Chapter Tests, Form D

The Form D Chapter Tests in this resource are composed of large mathematical tasks which allow students to demonstrate a broad spectrum of their abilities:

- how they reason through difficult problems;
- how they make and test conjectures;
- how their number sense helps them give reasonable answers;
- how they utilize alternative strategies.

These performance tasks also give teachers a means of assessing qualities of imagination, creativity, and perseverance.

Administering Form D Tests

Below are some classroom management tips for using the Form D tests.

- Whenever possible, use Form D Tests as cooperative group activities, listening as students interact in their groups.
- Have any needed mathematical tools or manipulatives readily available. The use of calculators is assumed.
- Ask students questions that will give you information about their thought processes.
- Be sure all students understand the purpose of the task. Offer assistance as needed.

Evaluating Form D Tests

For each Form D test, a set of task-specific performance standards (i.e., a general rubric or set of item-specific rubrics) provides a means for judging the quality of the students' work. These standards identify five levels of performance related to the particular task. The specific standards were created using the following characteristics of student performance as general guidelines.

Level 5: Accomplishes and extends the task; displays in-depth understanding; communicates effectively and completely.

Level 4: Accomplishes the task competently; displays clear understanding of key concepts; communicates effectively.

Level 3: Substantially completes the task; displays minor flaws in understanding or technique; communicates successfully.

Level 2: Only partially completes the task; displays one or more major errors in understanding or technique; communicates unclear or incomplete information.

Level 1: Attempts the task, but fails to complete it in any substantive way; displays only fragmented understanding; attempts communication, but is not successful.

Notice that this set of criteria is slightly varied from the set of criteria provided in the section on rubrics. In these criteria, there are three levels that would likely be considered successful (3, 4, and 5).

Each test is accompanied by a set of teacher notes that identifies the chapter objectives being assessed, as well as the mathematical concepts and skills involved in the performance task. The notes also list any materials that are needed and provide answers where appropriate. Questions to guide students as they seek solutions are provided, along with ideas for extending the activity. These notes, along with the performance standards as described at the left, are found in the Evaluation Guides starting on page A15 of this resource.

Because performance tasks are open-ended, student responses are as varied and individual as the students themselves. For this reason, it may be helpful to use these general guidelines as well as the task-specific standards when determining the level of each student's performance.

Assigning Writing Tasks

You might consider using writing for several purposes throughout the year.

Mathematics Autobiographies

At the beginning of the year, you might have students write a mathematics autobiography, in which they discuss their mathematics history and their expectations for the year (Countryman 1992). Mathematics autobiographies can provide insight into your students' backgrounds, attitudes, and perspectives. These insights can help you build a classroom environment that is conducive to learning. Rather than assigning a grade to these autobiographies, you might simply assess them as complete or incomplete.

Writing for Formative Purposes

Throughout the year, you might assign writing tasks for formative purposes, to determine what students understand and what misconceptions they hold, so you can modify instruction. These can be very short writing assessments such as the following:

- Tell me one thing you understand about today's lesson.
- Write one question you still have about today's lesson.
- Suppose a friend is absent today. Write a letter explaining to your friend what he or she missed.
- To review for a quiz or test, identify the most important concepts you should know from Lessons X through Y.

As with the autobiographies, you might give credit solely for completion.

Writing on Quizzes and Tests

There are some items on the quizzes and tests in this resource that incorporate writing into the solution. You can incorporate more writing into quizzes and tests by including items that ask students to write about their solutions. Such items are becoming increasingly important, as many states are including them on their high-stakes assessments.

Items from the Form C tests are good choices to be included on tests or quizzes. Even if you do not want to administer an entire Form C test, you might include items from that form on the Form A or B test or on quizzes.

If your state has a published rubric for scoring performance assessments, we encourage you to use that rubric for scoring such items. This allows students to become accustomed to the quality of response needed for each score level. (General information about rubrics is provided on page viii. Specific criteria for scoring items on the Forms C and D test are provided in the answers.)

To improve their writing, students need to see a variety of responses. You might have students work in groups to critique responses of students from a different class. (Do not reveal the names of the students whose writing they are critiquing.) Students can use the state rubric to determine what score they would assign to a response, providing a rationale for their decision. As students see poor responses, they can determine what needs to be done to improve the response. As they see high-quality or model responses, they can be encouraged to write similar responses.

Many students are not accustomed to writing in mathematics. There are many benefits for students and teachers in the writing process. However, it may take time to help students learn to write quality responses.

Caution: Writing tasks take time to complete. Teachers should carefully consider the number of writing items to include on a given assessment. Unless you are giving the entire Form C assessment, we suggest no more than one or two writing tasks on a given test. You might give students writing assessments for formative purposes (a problem or two at the end of class or as part of homework) two or three times per week.

Oral Presentations

Oral presentations provide another avenue for students to explain their thinking. Oral presentations might be as simple as having a student write a solution to a problem on the board and explain that solution to the class. Such presentations could be considered formative assessments and not graded in any way.

More formal oral presentations, such as presentations of projects, can be scored using a rubric or specific set of criteria. It is important that students be aware of the grading criteria prior to their presentations. A form for assessing oral presentations is provided in this resource.

Some teachers allow students to assess each other's presentations. This reinforces the presentation criteria and encourages students to pay attention during the presentations. A form for students to assess their classmates' presentations is provided in this resource.

Using Assessment Forms

Using Student-Completed Forms

Self Assessments

To do meaningful work in our fast-paced and ever-changing technological world, students must learn to assess their own progress. This resource provides four forms to help students with self-assessment.

Assessment of Other Students

You may wish to have students present their work on projects or other performance tasks orally to the class. This resource includes a form students can use to evaluate their classmates' presentations.

Using Teacher-Completed Forms

This resource provides forms designed to help you keep a record of assessments. Some forms are for use with individual students, while others are for use with groups of students. Determine which would be best suited for use in your classroom.

	Form	Purpose	Suggested Uses
Student-Completed	*Student Survey*	Checklist of student attitudes toward various math activities	• Periodically monitor the change in student attitudes toward math
	Student Self-Assessment	Checklist of student awareness of how well he or she works independently	• Monitor student progress in working independently on specific tasks
	Cooperative Groups Self-Assessment	Form for students to describe their attitudes and interaction with other students in a cooperative-learning situation	• Completed at the conclusion of group learning activities • Completed by individual students or groups of students
	About My Portfolio	Form for student to describe the contents of his or her portfolio	• Completed when student transfers work to the portfolio
	Evaluation of Classmate's Oral Presentation	Form for students to evaluate an oral presentation by a classmate.	• Completed after an oral presentation
Teacher-Completed	*Portfolio Assessment*	Form to assess student's mathematical accomplishments over time	• Use to discuss student's progress in discussions with family
	Notebooks, Individual Assessment	Form to record student's organizational skills and completeness of assignments	• Describe student's attention to specified daily tasks
	Notebooks, Class Checklist	Checklist to record students' notebook maintenance	• Use when setting goals for improving study skills
	Problem Solving, Individual Assessment	Form to assess each student in a problem-solving situation	• Describe level of student performance • Modify the level to meet individual needs
	Problem Solving, Class Checklist	Checklist to assess groups of students in problem-solving situations	• Assess the entire class • Assess small groups over time
	Observation, Individual Assessment	Form to determine the student's thought processes, performances, and attitudes	• Record observation of student in classroom
	Observation, Class Checklist	Checklist for observing several students at one time	• Provide a mathematical profile of the entire class • Identify common strengths and weaknesses • Help in modifying content or pace and in determining appropriate groupings
	Cooperative Groups, Class Checklist	Checklist to assess students' abilities to work constructively in groups	• Assess one or more cooperative groups
	Project Assessment	Form for evaluating extended projects or oral presentations	• Evaluate an individual or group project or presentation • Prepare students for presentations or projects
	Overall Student Assessment, Class Checklist	Checklist summary of students' overall performance	• Evaluate student performance over an entire instructional period

Student Survey

Answer the following questions using the rating scale provided.

5 Always
4 Usually
3 Sometimes
2 Rarely
1 Never

_____ **1.** I read material more than once if I don't understand it.

_____ **2.** I use the reading heads and bold terms to help me preview the material.

_____ **3.** I review for a test more than one day before it is given.

_____ **4.** I concentrate when I study.

_____ **5.** I try all the examples.

_____ **6.** I do all of my assigned homework.

_____ **7.** I pay attention in class.

_____ **8.** I take notes and keep my notebook up-to-date and neat.

_____ **9.** I bring the required materials to class.

_____ **10.** I really try to get good grades.

_____ **11.** I ask questions and try to get help when I need it.

_____ **12.** I use the Self-Test and Chapter Review to prepare for tests.

_____ **13.** I make up work when I have been absent.

_____ **14.** I like uses of math in real life.

_____ **15.** I can solve most problems.

_____ **16.** I like to try new strategies.

_____ **17.** I give up too easily.

_____ **18.** I work well cooperatively.

My favorite kind of math is _____

because _____

List some activities in which you have used math.

_____

_____

_____

Of the items listed above, what do you need to work on now? _____

_____

What was your favorite part of math class during this last grading period? _____

_____

What was your least favorite part of math class during this last grading period? _____

_____

Student Self-Assessment

Assignment

Complete the following sentences to describe your learning experience.

I was supposed to learn _____

_____

I started the work by _____

_____

_____

As a group member, I contributed _____

_____

_____

I learned _____

_____

_____

I am still confused by _____

_____

_____

I enjoyed the assignment because _____

_____

_____

I think the assignment was worthwhile because _____

_____

_____

Check the sentences that describe your work on this assignment.

☐ I was able to do the work.

☐ I did not understand the directions.

☐ I followed the directions but got wrong answers.

☐ I can explain how to do this assignment to someone else.

☐ The assignment was easier than I thought it would be.

☐ The assignment was harder than I thought it would be.

Cooperative Groups Self-Assessment

Assignment

Reader: *Writer:*

Materials handler: *Checker:*

Others in group:

Materials:

Check the sentences that describe your group's work.

- ☐ We had a new idea or made a suggestion.
- ☐ We asked for more information.
- ☐ We shared the information we found.
- ☐ We tried different ways to solve the problem.
- ☐ We helped others explain their ideas better.
- ☐ We pulled our ideas together.
- ☐ We were reminded to work together.
- ☐ We demonstrated a knowledge of the mathematical concept.
- ☐ We encouraged those who did not understand.

Complete each sentence.

We learned

We found an answer by

After we found an answer, we

By working together, we

About My Portfolio

Complete the following sentences about the work you are putting into your portfolio.

Describe the assignment.

_____

_____

_____

I chose this work as part of my portfolio because

_____

_____

_____

I began my work by

_____

_____

_____

Doing this work helped me

_____

_____

_____

The work was ☐ too easy ☐ easy ☐ just right ☐ hard ☐ too hard

because _____

_____

_____

Evaluation of Classmates' Oral Presentation

Circle the appropiate number in each category. The lower end of the scale is a *poor* rating and the right end of the scale is an *excellent* rating.

Name(s)										
Relevant and easy-to-read visuals	2	4	6	8	10	2	4	6	8	10
Organization/Flow	1	2	3	4	5	1	2	3	4	5
Creativity	1	2	3	4	5	1	2	3	4	5
Eye contact	1	2	3	4	5	1	2	3	4	5
Voice projection	1	2	3	4	5	1	2	3	4	5
Working with visuals	1	2	3	4	5	1	2	3	4	5
Professionalism/appearance	1	2	3	4	5	1	2	3	4	5
Content	2	4	6	8	10	2	4	6	8	10

Portfolio Assessment

The work in this portfolio:

shows growth in the student's mathematical understanding.

exhibits the student's ability to reason mathematically.

makes connections within mathematics.

makes connections to other disciplines.

shows that the student is able to work on mathematical tasks in cooperative groups.

illustrates the appropriate use of a variety of tools.

Notebooks

Rate items, based upon your requirements, as follows:

+	if excellent
✓	if satisfactory
–	if needs improvement
NA	if not applicable

Written Assignments

Comments

_____ 1. Assignment sheet

_____ 2. Daily homework

_____ 3. Lesson Warm-Ups

_____ 4. Lesson Masters

_____ 5. Activities

_____ 6. Projects

Reading and Class Notes

Comments

_____ 7. Definitions

_____ 8. Properties

_____ 9. Examples

_____ 10. Class notes, handouts

Formal Assessment

Comments

_____ 11. Chapter Quizzes

_____ 12. Chapter Self-Test

_____ 13. Chapter Review

_____ 14. Chapter Tests

_____ 15. Cumulative Chapter Test

_____ 16. Comprehensive Test

Other

Comments

_____ 17.

_____ 18.

_____ 19.

_____ 20.

Overall Rating/Comments

Notebooks   Class Checklist

Class

Rate each item as follows:

+	if excellent
✓	if satisfactory
–	if needs improvement
NA	if not applicable

Student	Date	Written Assignments		Reading/Class Notes		Assessment					
1.											
2.											
3.											
4.											
5.											
6.											
7.											
8.											
9.											
10.											
11.											
12.											
13.											
14.											
15.											
16.											
17.											
18.											
19.											
20.											
21.											
22.											
23.											
24.											
25.											
26.											
27.											
28.											
29.											
30.											

Problem Solving

Check each statement below that accurately describes the student's work. This list includes suggested student behaviors to consider. Feel free to modify it to suit your needs.

Reads Carefully   **Comments**

☐ Looks up unfamiliar words

☐ Understands lesson concepts and can apply them

☐ Rereads

☐ Finds/uses information appropriately

☐

☐

☐

Creates a plan   **Comments**

☐ Chooses an appropriate strategy

☐ Estimates the answer

☐

☐

☐

Carries out the plan   **Comments**

☐ Works systematically and with care

☐ Shows work in an organized fashion

☐ Computes correctly

☐ Rereads the problem if the first attempt at a solution is unsuccessful

☐ Rereads the problem and interprets the solution

☐ States the answer in required or appropiate format

☐

☐

☐

Checks the work   **Comments**

☐ Checks by estimating

☐ Tries alternate approaches

☐

☐

☐

Problem Solving

Class

Rate each item as follows:

+	if excellent
✓	if satisfactory
–	if needs improvement
NA	if not applicable

Student	Date	Tries alternate approaches	States answer in required format	Rereads the problem if necessary	Computes correctly	Checks the answer	Estimates the answer	Chooses an appropriate strategy	Uses information appropriately	Understands the question/task	Looks up unfamiliar words
1.											
2.											
3.											
4.											
5.											
6.											
7.											
8.											
9.											
10.											
11.											
12.											
13.											
14.											
15.											
16.											
17.											
18.											
19.											
20.											
21.											
22.											
23.											
24.											
25.											
26.											
27.											
28.											
29.											
30.											

Observation

	Usually	Sometimes	Rarely
Understanding			
Demonstrates knowledge of skills	☐	☐	☐
Understands concepts	☐	☐	☐
Selects appropriate solution strategies	☐	☐	☐
Solves problems accurately	☐	☐	☐
Work Habits			
Works in an organized manner	☐	☐	☐
Works neatly	☐	☐	☐
Submits work on time	☐	☐	☐
Works well with others	☐	☐	☐
Uses time productively	☐	☐	☐
Asks for help when needed	☐	☐	☐
Confidence			
Initiates questions	☐	☐	☐
Displays positive attitude	☐	☐	☐
Helps others	☐	☐	☐
Flexibility			
Tries alternative approaches	☐	☐	☐
Considers and uses ideas of others	☐	☐	☐
Likes to try alternative methods	☐	☐	☐
Perseverance			
Shows patience and perseverance	☐	☐	☐
Works systematically	☐	☐	☐
Is willing to try	☐	☐	☐
Checks work regularly	☐	☐	☐
Other			
_____	☐	☐	☐
_____	☐	☐	☐
_____	☐	☐	☐

Observation

Class

Rate each item as follows:

+	if excellent
✓	if satisfactory
–	if needs improvement
NA	if not applicable

Student	Date	Shows patience and perseverance	Considers and uses ideas of others	Tries alternative approaches	Displays positive attitude	Uses time productively	Asks for help when needed	Works well with others	Works neatly and systematically	Understands concepts	Demonstrates knowledge of skills
1.											
2.											
3.											
4.											
5.											
6.											
7.											
8.											
9.											
10.											
11.											
12.											
13.											
14.											
15.											
16.											
17.											
18.											
19.											
20.											
21.											
22.											
23.											
24.											
25.											
26.											
27.											
28.											
29.											
30.											

Cooperative Groups

Class

Rate each item as follows:

+	if excellent
✓	if satisfactory
–	if needs improvement
NA	if not applicable

Student	Date	Uses reasonable voice volume	Works with others in the group	Considers and uses ideas of others	Tutors and helps others	Has a positive attitude	Disagrees but is not disagreeable	Shows patience and perseverance	Works systematically	Initiates questions	
1.											
2.											
3.											
4.											
5.											
6.											
7.											
8.											
9.											
10.											
11.											
12.											
13.											
14.											
15.											
16.											
17.											
18.											
19.											
20.											
21.											
22.											
23.											
24.											
25.											
26.											
27.											
28.											
29.											
30.											

Project Assignment

Rate each item as follows:

+	if excellent
✓	if satisfactory
–	if needs improvement
NA	if not applicable

The Project

_____ Demonstrates mathematical concepts properly

_____ Communicates ideas clearly

_____ Shows connection to another subject

_____ Shows evidence of time spent in planning and preparation

_____ Is original and creative

_____ Includes charts, tables, and/or graphs where appropriate

_____ Uses available technology effectively

_____ Stimulates further investigation of the topic

_____ Includes a short written report if the project is a model or demonstration

_____ Lists resources used

The Oral Presentation

_____ Is organized (includes an introduction, main section, and conclusion)

_____ Uses audio-visual materials where appropriate

_____ Speaks clearly and paces presentation properly

_____ Answers questions and stimulates further interest among classmates

_____ Holds audience's attention

Overall Project Rating/Comments

_____

_____

_____

_____

Name _____   **Date** _____

Overall Student Assessment

Class _____

Rate each item as follows:

+	if excellent
✓	if satisfactory
–	if needs improvement
NA	if not applicable

Student	Date	Class work	Discussion	Cooperative Groups	Problem Solving	Homework	Notebooks	Projects	Quizzes	Tests	Lab Work
1.											
2.											
3.											
4.											
5.											
6.											
7.											
8.											
9.											
10.											
11.											
12.											
13.											
14.											
15.											
16.											
17.											
18.											
19.											
20.											
21.											
22.											
23.											
24.											
25.											
26.											
27.											
28.											
29.											
30.											

References

Carter, John A. & Dorothy E. Carter. *The Write Equation: Writing in the Mathematics Classroom.* Palo Alto, CA: Dale Seymour Publications, 1994.

Countryman, Joan. *Writing to Learn Mathematics: Strategies That Work, K-12.* Portsmouth, NH: Heinemann, 1992.

National Council of Teachers of Mathematics. *Principles and Standards for School Mathematics.* Reston, VA: National Council of Teachers of Mathematics, 2000.

Thompson, Denisse R. & Sharon L. Senk. "Using Rubrics in High School Mathematics." *Mathematics Teacher, 91* (December 1998): 786-793.

Quiz Lessons 1-1 through 1-4

1. Show that 641 millionths is rational by writing it as the ratio of two integers.

   1. _____

2. Identify **a.** the rate and **b.** the rate unit in the following sentence:

   In 1990, the population density of Juniata County, Pennsylvania, was 20.3 people per square mile.

   2. a. _____

   b. _____

3. **Multiple Choice** Which of the following statements correctly compares −18.3, −18.9, and 18.7?

   A −18.3 < −18.9 < 18.7   B −18.9 > 18.7 > −18.3

   C 18.7 > −18.3 > −18.9   D −18.9 < 18.7 > −18.3

   3. _____

4. A *score* is a count equal to twenty. Use this information to identify **a.** the count *and* **b.** the counting unit in the following passage:

   "Four score and seven years ago, our fathers brought forth on this continent a new nation, conceived in liberty and dedicated to the proposition that all men are created equal."

   Abraham Lincoln, *Gettysburg Address,* November 19, 1863

   4. a. _____

   b. _____

5. Is the underlined number in the following sentence used as an identification, a count, or a measure?

   On July 4, 1939, the New York Yankees retired Lou Gehrig's uniform number 4.

   5. _____

6. Evaluate four to the sixth power.

   6. _____

7. Compare 3^5 and 5^3, using <, >, or =.

   7. _____

8. On the number line below, which letter corresponds to 3.8?

   8. _____

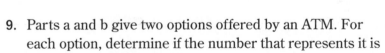

9. Parts a and b give two options offered by an ATM. For each option, determine if the number that represents it is positive, negative, or zero.

   a. Deposit money.

   9. a. _____

   b. Withdraw money.

   b. _____

Quiz Lessons 1-5 through 1-8

1. **a.** What is the first operation to perform in evaluating the following expression?

   $8.3 \times (4 + 6 \div 7.5) - 8.1$

   b. Evaluate the expression.

   1. **a.** _____

   b. _____

2. Most gold-plated jewelry sold in the United States has a coating of gold that is about 3.5 millionths of a meter thick. Write this number in scientific notation.

   2. _____

3. **Multiple Choice** Which of the following expresses 568,000,000,000 in scientific notation?

   A 5.68×10^9

   B 568×10^9

   C 568×10^{11}

   D 5.68×10^{11}

   3. _____

In 4–6, evaluate.

4. $\dfrac{64 - \sqrt{8^2 + 18 \cdot 2}}{11 - 9 + 2}$

   4. _____

5. $15^2 + 9 \cdot 2$

   5. _____

6. $a^2 + (b - a) \cdot a$, when $a = 2$ and $b = 7$

   6. _____

7. **a.** Write a calculator key sequence for evaluating $\dfrac{(2 + 5)^3}{16 - \sqrt{162 \div 2}}$.

   7. **a.** _____

   _____

   b. Evaluate the expression.

   b. _____

In 8 and 9, write $<$, $>$, or $=$ to make a true sentence.

8. $(29 - 2) \cdot (52 + 7) \underline{\quad ? \quad} 29 - 2 \cdot 52 + 7$

   8. _____

9. $10^{-3} \underline{\quad ? \quad} 10^{-4}$

   9. _____

10. Write one ten-thousandth as

   a. a decimal.

   b. a power of ten.

   c. a fraction.

   10. **a.** _____

   b. _____

   c. _____

11. **Fill in the Blanks** To multiply a number by $\dfrac{1}{100,000,000,000}$ move the decimal point $\underline{\ ?\ }$ spaces to the $\underline{\ ?\ }$.

   11. _____

   _____

Chapter 1 Test Form A

In 1–3, evaluate the expression, showing each step of the order of operations.

1. $4^3 - 5 \cdot 2$

1. _____

2. $12^0 + \dfrac{8+3}{4 \cdot 22}$

2. _____

3. $\sqrt{9} - 2 \cdot (4+6)$

3. _____

In 4–6, use the table below, which shows the U.S. goods trade deficit with China for the first five months of 2005.

Month	Trade Deficit (millions of dollars)
January	15,276.5
February	13,829.5
March	12,848.6
April	14,776.6
May	15,816.4

4. Write a double inequality comparing the trade deficits in February, March, and April.

4. _____

5. Plot and label the trade deficits for January and March, in billions of dollars, on the number line at the right.

5.
9   11   13   15   17

6. Convert the dollar value for May into scientific notation.

6. _____

In 7 and 8, consider the expression 429.3×10^8.

7. Is this number in scientific notation? Explain why or why not.

7. _____

_____

8. Multiply the expression by $\dfrac{1}{10,000}$. Write the result in base-10 notation.

8. _____

9. a. Write a calculator key sequence for evaluating $\dfrac{\sqrt{100}+8}{3^2}$.

9. a. _____

   b. Evaluate the expression.

   b. _____

In 10 and 11, use the scatterplot below.

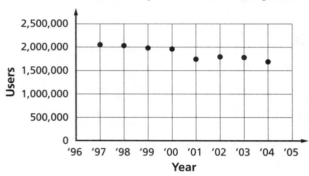

New York Public Library—Research Library Users

10. Estimate the number of Research Library users that visited the New York Public Library in 1999.

10. _____

11. What window dimensions and scale were used for this scatterplot?

11. _____

_____

12. **Multiple Choice** Which number is not rational?

   A 5^0 B $\frac{7}{0}$ C $\frac{9.6}{2}$ D $\sqrt{0}$

12. _____

13. Use the grid to help you fill in the table at the right.

13.

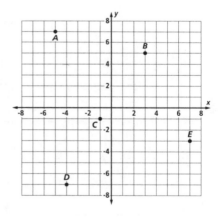

Point	Ordered Pair	Quadrant
A	a. (,)	f.
B	b. (,)	g.
C	c. (,)	h.
D	d. (,)	i.
E	e. (,)	j.

14. Write each number as a decimal.

   a. 4.5^3

14. a. _____

   b. 2.3 trillion

   b. _____

   c. sixteen and seventeen millionths

   c. _____

15. Consider the following sentence:

    Jamie bought five pairs of shoes on Wednesday.

    a. Identify the count.

    b. Identify the counting unit.

16. Identify the underlined number as one of the following:

    i   a rate   ii   an identification

    iii   a comparison   iv   a count

    a. Sponge cake takes <u>twice</u> as long to bake as oatmeal cookies.

    b. The hot-air balloon traveled north at about <u>20</u> miles per hour.

17. Multiply 70.81 by

    a. 10^{-6}.

    b. 100,000,000.

    c. $\frac{1}{10^4}$.

    d. 0.000001.

18. Use a calculator to evaluate $15^8 - 14^8$.

19. In a skyscraper, would you describe the following floors with a positive integer, a negative integer, or zero?

    a. the ground floor

    b. the penthouse, eighty floors up from ground level

    c. the sub-basement, two stories below the ground

20. Write $<$, $>$, or $=$ to make a true sentence.

    a. 5.6×10^{-3} __?__ 0.056

    b. $18 + 2^1$ __?__ $\sqrt{400}$

15. a. _____

    b. _____

16. a. _____

    b. _____

17. a. _____

    b. _____

    c. _____

    d. _____

18. _____

19. a. _____

    b. _____

    c. _____

20. a. _____

    b. _____

Chapter 1 Test   Form B

In 1–3, evaluate the expression, showing each step of the order of operations.

1. $3^4 + 4 \cdot 2$

1. _____

2. $8^0 + \dfrac{11 + 7}{6 \cdot 12}$

2. _____

3. $\sqrt{25} - 3 \cdot (8 - 2)$

3. _____

In 4–6, use the table below, which shows the U.S. goods trade deficit with China for the last five months of 2005.

Month	Trade Deficit (millions of dollars)
August	18,532.6
September	20,085.4
October	20,435.3
November	18,536.1
December	16,221.0

4. Write a double inequality comparing the trade deficits in September, October, and November.

4. _____

5. Plot and label the trade deficits for November and December, in billions of dollars, on the number line at the right.

5.
15   17   19   21   23

6. Convert the dollar value for August into scientific notation.

6. _____

In 7 and 8, consider the expression 614.9×10^7.

7. Is this number in scientific notation? Explain.

7. _____

8. Multiply the expression by $\dfrac{1}{10,000}$. Write the result in base-10 notation.

8. _____

9. a. Write a calculator key sequence for evaluating $\dfrac{4 + \sqrt{64}}{2^2}$.

9. a. _____

   b. Evaluate the expression.

   b. _____

Chapter 1 Test Form B

In 10 and 11, use the scatterplot.

New York Public Library—Research Library Users

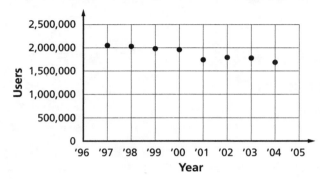

10. Estimate the number of Research Library users that visited the New York Public Library in 2002.

10. _____

11. What window dimensions and scale were used for this scatterplot?

11. _____

_____

12. **Multiple Choice** Which of the following is not a rational number?

12. _____

A $\sqrt{0}$ B $\frac{11.7}{3}$ C 3^0 D $\frac{4}{0}$

13. Use the grid to help you fill in the table at the right.

13.

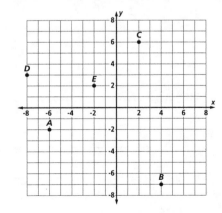

Point	Ordered Pair	Quadrant
A	a. (,)	f.
B	b. (,)	g.
C	c. (,)	h.
D	d. (,)	i.
E	e. (,)	j.

14. Write each number as a decimal.

a. 6.5^4

14. a. _____

b. 7.32 billion

b. _____

c. fourteen and twenty millionths

c. _____

Chapter 1 Test   Form B

15. Consider the following sentence:

    Jamie bought three cans of tennis balls on Saturday.

    a. Identify the count.

    b. Identify the counting unit.

15. a. _____

    b. _____

16. Identify the underlined number as one of the following:

    i   a rate   ii   an identification

    iii   a comparison   iv   a count

    a. Anne put her gym clothes in locker 323.

    b. Ms. Molina's car gets an average of 27 miles per gallon of gas.

16. a. _____

    b. _____

17. Multiply 62.43 by

    a. 10^{-7}.

    b. 10,000,000.

    c. $\frac{1}{10^3}$.

    d. 0.00000001.

17. a. _____

    b. _____

    c. _____

    d. _____

18. Use a calculator to evaluate $12^9 - 11^9$.

18. _____

19. Would you describe the following elevations with a positive number, a negative number, or zero?

    a. 283 feet below sea level, the elevation of Death Valley, California

    b. sea level

    c. 20,320 feet above sea level, the elevation of the highest point on Denali in Alaska

19. a. _____

    b. _____

    c. _____

20. Write <, >, or = to make a true sentence.

    a. 2.1×10^{-4} ___?___ 0.00021

    b. $4^3 \div 2$ ___?___ $\sqrt{900}$

20. a. _____

    b. _____

Chapter 1 Test Form C

1. Explain how you know that 7.25 is a rational number. Then, write a sentence in which this number is used as a rate and a sentence in which it is used as a measure.

2. Which of these numbers are equal? Which number is in scientific notation? Explain your answers.

   89.7 millionths   0.000897

   89.7×10^{-7} 8.97×10^{-5}

3. Evaluate the expression below without using a calculator. Then, write a sentence that uses the result as a count and a sentence that uses it as a code or location.

   $$72 - 36 \div 3^2 \times 5$$

4. Maria has $6.50. Frida owes $2.25. Elena owes $3.00.
   Fill in the blanks to compare the three amounts, writing them as positive and negative numbers.

   _____ < _____ < _____

   Draw a number line and plot points for the three numbers.

5. Evaluate 4.8^5 by using your calculator. Then, without actually multiplying, tell what power of 10 you would need to multiply the result by to move the digit 4 to the millions place. Explain how you found your answer.

6. Explain how you can determine what quadrant a point is in simply by looking at its ordered pair. If you are told a point is not in any quadrant, what can you say about its ordered pair? Explain.

Chapter 1 Test Form D

You are a writer for a national magazine. Your assignment is to write an article comparing the education levels reached by males and females in the United States over the past 30 years. While doing your research, you find the scatterplot and table below. The plot shows the number of bachelor's degrees earned by males in the United States for selected years since 1977. The table shows similar data for females.

Bachelor's Degrees Earned by Females

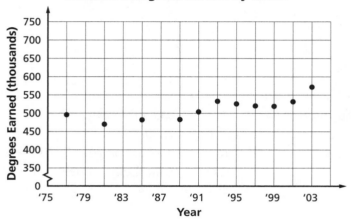

Bachelor's Degrees Earned by Males

Year	Degrees Earned (thousands)
1977	424
1981	465
1985	497
1989	535
1991	590
1993	632
1995	634
1997	652
1999	682
2001	712
2003	775

Source: National Center for Education Statistics

a. Using a different color or plot symbol, add the data for females to the plot.

b. Use the information in the finished scatterplot to write a paragraph or two for your article. Be sure to include the following:

- A description of the overall trend in the number of bachelor's degrees awarded to males.

- A description of the overall trend in the number of bachelor's degrees awarded to females.

- A comparison of the data for females and the data for males.

- A prediction about the bachelor's degrees that will be awarded in 2013.

Quiz   Lessons 2-1 through 2-3

In 1 and 2, translate into an algebraic expression.

1. seventeen less the square of a number

    1. _____

2. 180 multiplied by the sum of a and b

    2. _____

3. Three instances of a pattern are given. Describe the general pattern using one variable.

    1 pound of pasta makes 8 servings.

    2 pounds of pasta make 16 servings.

    5 pounds of pasta make 40 servings.

    3. _____

4. A laundromat charges customers $1.50 to wash a load of laundry. Fill in the table relating the number of loads to the cost.

    4.

Number of Loads	Cost
1	$1.50
2	
3	
4	
5	
n	

5. Three instances of a pattern are given. Describe the general pattern using one variable.

    $$(7 + 9) \cdot 5 = 7 \cdot 5 + 9 \cdot 5$$

    $$(7 + 2.2) \cdot 5 = 7 \cdot 5 + 2.2 \cdot 5$$

    $$(7 + \sqrt{17}) \cdot 5 = 7 \cdot 5 + \sqrt{17} \cdot 5$$

    5. _____

6. Evaluate $34.8 - x^3$ when $x = 3.1$.

    6. _____

7. Evaluate $\dfrac{16 + j}{j^2}$ when $j = 0.7$.

    7. _____

8. Give three instances of the pattern
    $4 + (c + 9) = (4 + c) + 9$.

    8. _____

    _____

    _____

9. Suppose your family's electric bill for November is D dollars. Write an expression for the December electric bill if it is $30 more than the November bill.

    9. _____

Name _____

1. Find the value of *c* in the right triangle below.

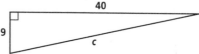

1. _____

2. **Multiple Choice** Which of the following could *not* be the lengths of the sides of a right triangle?

    A 17, 15, 8

    C 5, 16, 13

    B 7, 25, 24

    D 12, 20, 16

2. _____

3. If the sales tax rate is 6%, then the total cost *S* of an item priced at *c* dollars is $S = 1.06c$. What is the total cost of a pair of pants priced at \$24.99?

3. _____

4. The legs of a right triangle measure 32 inches and 60 inches. Find the length of the hypotenuse.

4. _____

5. A formula for the perimeter *P* of a square is $P = 4s$, where *s* is the length of a side of the square. Find the perimeter of a square with a side of length 800 units.

5. _____

6. **a.** Write a spreadsheet formula that will compute the average of the values in cells A6, C7, and D4.

6. a. _____

    b. Evaluate your formula from Part a if the value in cell A6 is 24, the value in cell C7 is 70, and the value in cell D4 is 92.

    b. _____

7. **True or False** The tent pictured below can be set up in a clearing that is 3 meters wide. Justify your answer.

7. _____

Chapter 2 Test Form A

1. **Multiple Choice** If $15(x + 4) = 135$, then $x =$ _____?_____.

    A 4   B 9

    C 6   D 5

    1. _____

2. **Multiple Choice** When $j = 0$, $k = 14$, and $l = 5$, then $\dfrac{(17 + jk^3) - (k - j^3)}{3l + j} =$ _____?_____.

    A 0   B $\dfrac{3}{5}$

    C 1   D $\dfrac{1}{5}$

    2. _____

3. Evaluate $4p + b - (4 - bp)^2$ when $b = 2$ and $p = 1.5$.

    3. _____

4. A corner market will deliver produce for a flat rate of $2.00, plus the cost of the produce. Using this information, fill in the table at the right.

    4.

Number of Honeydew Melons	Cost (including delivery)
1	$7.99
2	$13.98
7	a.
10	$61.90
12	b.
100	c.

5. Using the table from Question 4, write a formula for the cost C (including delivery) of m honeydew melons.

    5. _____

6. Three instances of a pattern are given. Describe the pattern using one variable.

    One can of soup has 120 calories.

    Two cans of soup have 240 calories.

    Seven cans of soup have 840 calories.

    6. _____

7. Give three instances of the following pattern.

    $\dfrac{a}{b} + \dfrac{c}{d} = \dfrac{ad + cb}{bd}$

    7. _____

    _____

    _____

8. Write the following as an algebraic expression: fifteen less a number, then the difference raised to the third power.

    8. _____

9. Below are three instances of a pattern. Describe the general pattern using two variables.

    $5.3 \times 10^{-5} = 5.3 \times \frac{1}{10^5}$

    $7.01 \times 10^{-7} = 7.01 \times \frac{1}{10^7}$

    $2.56 \times 10^{-1} = 2.56 \times \frac{1}{10^1}$

9. _____

In 10 and 11, graph all solutions to the sentence.

10. $q \geq -2.5$

11. $-1 < t < 0$

10.

11.

12. This spreadsheet gives information about the world land-speed records set at a 1 km course at Bonneville Flats, Utah.

	A	B	C	D
1	**Driver (Year)**	**Old Record (mph)**	**New Record (mph)**	**Difference**
2	John Cobb (1939)	357.33	369.74	12.41
3	John Cobb (1947)	369.74	393.82	24.08
4	Craig Breedlove (1963)	393.82	408.312	
5	Tom Green (1964)	408.312	415.093	
6	Art Arfons (1964)	415.093	434.356	
7	**Average Change in Record:**			

a. Give the formulas that should be entered in cells D4, D5, and D6. Also give the values that will appear in those cells after the formulas are entered.

12. a. _____

_____

_____

b. The average difference between records will be displayed in cell D7. Write a formula for this cell.

b. _____

13. Find the solution of $98.1 + j = 108.1$.

13. _____

14. Evaluate $\frac{a^3 - 17(a - b)}{ab}$ when $a = 3$ and $b = 1$.

14. _____

Name _____

15. On the map below, Ash Street and Elm Street intersect
    at a right angle. What is the distance from the corner of
    Broadway and Ash to the corner of Broadway and Elm?

    15. _____

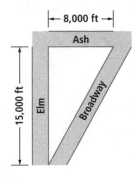

16. **Multiple Choice** A formula for the power used by an
    electrical appliance is $P = I^2R$, where P is the power
    (in watts), I is the current (in amperes), and R is the
    resistance (in ohms). What is the resistance in a 12-ampere
    vacuum cleaner that is using 1,440 Watts of power?

    16. _____

    A 8 ohms   B 10 ohms
    C 12 ohms   D 120 ohms

17. Are the numbers 20, 99, and 100 a Pythagorean triple?
    Justify your answer.

    17. _____

    _____

18. Find the length of the hypotenuse of the right triangle with
    legs of length 48 and 55.

    18. _____

19. Solve for b: $\frac{1}{2}b = 320$.

    19. _____

20. Use the table at the right.

    a. Fill in the table.

    20. a.

Column 1	Column 2
1	3
2	5
3	7
4	
8	
10	
900	
n	

    b. Describe this pattern in words.

Chapter 2 Test Form B

1. **Multiple Choice** If $16(x + 5) = 128$, then $x =$ ____?____ .

   A 1   B 3

   C 6   D 8

   1. _____

2. **Multiple Choice** When $a = 15$, $b = 0$, and $c = 3$,

   then $\dfrac{(13 - a^2b^2) - (b^3 + c)}{5c + a} =$ ____?____ .

   A 0   B $\frac{1}{3}$

   C 1   D $\frac{2}{3}$

   2. _____

3. Evaluate $bp + 15 - (4p - b)^2$ when $b = 2$ and $p = 1.5$.

   3. _____

4. A corner market will deliver produce for a flat rate of
   $3.00, plus the cost of the produce. Using this information,
   fill in the table at right.

   4.

Pounds of Tomatoes	Cost (including delivery)
1	$5.29
2	$7.58
7	a.
10	$25.90
12	b.
100	c.

5. Using the table from Question 4, write a formula for the cost
   C (including delivery) of t pounds of tomatoes.

   5. _____

6. Three instances of a pattern are given. Describe the pattern
   using one variable.

   One spiral notebook has 180 sheets.

   Two spiral notebooks have 360 sheets.

   Seven spiral notebooks have 1260 sheets.

   6. _____

7. Give three instances of the following pattern.

   $\dfrac{a}{b} - \dfrac{c}{d} = \dfrac{ad - cb}{bd}$

   7. _____

   _____

   _____

8. Write the following as an algebraic expression: twelve less
   than a number, then the difference divided by nineteen.

   8. _____

Chapter 2 Test Form B

9. Below are three instances of a pattern. Describe the general pattern using two variables.

$\dfrac{4.82}{10^7} = 4.82 \times 10^{-7}$

$\dfrac{5.07}{10^2} = 5.07 \times 10^{-2}$

$\dfrac{9.3}{10^4} = 9.3 \times 10^{-4}$

9. _____

In 10 and 11, graph all solutions to the sentence.

10. $q < -1$

10.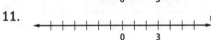

11. $-3 \le t < 1.5$

11.

12. WriteRight, Inc. sells paper, pens, and pencils. This spreadsheet shows last week's sales for the six WriteRight salespeople.

	A	B	C	D
1	Salesperson	Paper Sales	Writing Implement Sales	Total Sales
2	Tammy Merrit	$412.50	$198.00	$610.50
3	Victor Diaz	$295.00	$267.65	$562.65
4	Tamika Rashad	$389.25	$427.65	
5	Amy Cho	$215.00	$225.65	
6	Russell Lipinski	$642.75	$487.50	
7		Average Weekly Sales:		

a. Give the formulas that should be entered in cells D4, D5, and D6. Also give the values that will appear in these cells after the formulas are entered.

12. a. _____

_____

_____

b. The average total sales will be displayed in cell D7. Write a formula for this cell.

b. _____

13. Find the solution of $97.5 + j = 117.5$.

13. _____

14. Evaluate $\dfrac{b^4 - 12(a - b)}{3ab}$ when $a = 5$ and $b = 2$.

14. _____

Chapter 2 Test Form B

15. On the map below, Oak Street and Maple Street intersect at a right angle. What is the distance from the corner of Willow and Oak to the corner of Willow and Maple?

15. _____

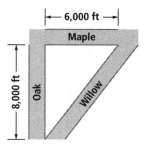

16. **Multiple Choice** A formula for the power used by an electrical appliance is $P = I^2R$, where P is the power (in watts), I is the current (in amperes), and R is the resistance (in ohms). What is the resistance in a 10-ampere vacuum cleaner that is using 1,300 Watts of power?

16. _____

A 10 ohms

B 1.3 ohms

C 13 ohms

D 130 ohms

17. Are the numbers 11, 30, and 32 a Pythagorean triple? Justify your answer.

17. _____

18. Find the length of the hypotenuse of the right triangle with legs of length 40 and 42.

18. _____

19. Solve for w: $\frac{1}{4}w = 120$.

19. _____

20. Use the table at the right.

   a. Fill in the table.

20. a.

Column 1	Column 2
1	1
2	3
3	5
4	
6	
10	
700	
n	

   b. Describe this pattern in words.

_____

Chapter 2 Test Form C

1. Evaluate $p^2 - 3$ when $p = 2$, $p = 3$, and $p = 4$. Which of these values are solutions of $p^2 - 3 = 10$? Which are solutions of $p^2 - 3 < 10$? Which are solutions of $p^2 - 3 \geq 10$? Explain your answers.

2. For each number line, write an inequality that describes the graph.

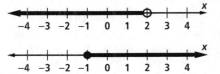

Graph the points that are on both number lines above and write a double inequality to describe the graph.

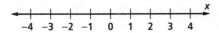

3. A soccer field is 90 m wide and 120 m long. Rafi ran along one edge, then along the adjacent edge, and then diagonally across the field. He repeated this several times. He claims he ran a total of 1600 m. Is this possible? Explain your answer.

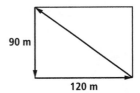

4. The table below gives the cost C for joining StayFit Gym for m months. The formula gives the cost for Roscoe's Gym. Which gym is less expensive for a one-year membership? (Assume the pattern in the table continues.) Explain your answer.

StayFit Gym

m	1	2	3	4	5
C	$60	$120	$180	$240	$300

Roscoe's Gym: $C = \$180 + \$40m$

5. Making a border around a 4 foot-by-6 foot pond using 1-foot-square tiles requires $2 \cdot 4 + 2 \cdot 6 + 4 = 24$ tiles. Making a border around a 5 foot-by-3 foot pond requires $2 \cdot 5 + 2 \cdot 3 + 4 = 20$ tiles. Give two more instances of this pattern. Then, write a description of the pattern using variables.

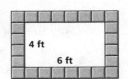

Chapter 2 Test Form D

You work in the school bookstore and are assigned to keep track of the items that are imprinted with the school name. Your school buys each item at a wholesale price W and sells it at a retail price R. You compute the school's profit P by using the formula $P = R - W$.

The chart at right gives the wholesale and retail prices for each school-imprint item that is sold in the bookstore.

a. Use the formula given above to complete the Profit column of the table.

b. What is the total amount of profit if you sell two T-shirts? Three T-shirts? Four T-shirts? Describe the pattern using variables.

c. Suppose you want to make a profit of exactly $65 from the sale of T-shirts. Write an equation you can solve to find the number of T-shirts you need to sell. What is the solution to your equation? How many T-shirts must you sell?

d. Suppose you want to make a profit of *at least* $50 from the sale of T-shirts. What is the least number of T-shirts you must sell? Explain your answer.

e. During the month of October, profits from the sale of all school-imprint items will be donated to the town scholarship fund. The goal is to donate a total of $1,500. The principal wants to focus on advertising and selling only a few items in order to reach this goal. Choose three or four items from the chart and show one way the bookstore could reach its goal by selling only these items. In other words, give estimates of the number of each item the store could sell in order to reach its goal. Write a memo to the principal that presents your estimates and any expressions, equations, and calculations you used to arrive at them. Include a graph that can be enlarged and placed on a poster to display your estimates in the school bookstore.

School-Imprint Items			
	Wholesale Price	Retail Price	Profit
Clothing			
T-shirts	$4.39	$6.99	
sweatshirts	$8.39	$12.99	
jackets	$21.69	$32.99	
caps	$6.99	$10.99	
Supplies			
notebooks	$1.29	$2.29	
3-ring binders	$2.69	$4.69	
pencils	39¢	69¢	
ball-point pens	69¢	$1.19	
decals	39¢	69¢	

Name _____

1. Find the value of $3^p + p^3$ when $p = 2$.

   1. _____

2. Find the value of $\dfrac{b(7-a)}{b+a^2}$ when $b = 6$ and $a = 2$.

   2. _____

3. Give two solutions of $6 - t > 2$

   3. _____

4. Find the solution of $6x = 54$.

   4. _____

5. Write the following as an algebraic expression: nine less the product of a number and four.

   5. _____

6. A right triangle has legs of length 16 feet and 30 feet. What is the length of the hypotenuse?

   6. _____

7. Are the numbers 20, 21, and 29 a Pythagorean triple? Justify your answer.

   7. _____

   _____

8. Three instances of a pattern are given. Describe the pattern using one variable.

   8. _____

   $\frac{3}{4} \cdot 8 = 8 - \frac{1}{4} \cdot 8$

   $\frac{3}{4} \cdot 32 = 32 - \frac{1}{4} \cdot 32$

   $\frac{3}{4} \cdot 4.8 = 4.8 - \frac{1}{4} \cdot 4.8$

9. Give two instances of the pattern $a - (b + c) = a - b - c$.

   9. _____

   _____

10. Three instances of a pattern are given. Use variables to describe the general pattern.

    10. _____

    Going to the fair and riding one ride costs $5 + 2 \cdot 1$ dollars.

    Going to the fair and riding six rides cost $5 + 2 \cdot 6$ dollars.

    Going to the fair and riding 12 rides cost $5 + 2 \cdot 12$ dollars.

11. Ted rode his scooter diagonally across an empty, rectangular parking lot. If the parking lot measures 45 yards by 60 yards, how far did Ted ride?

    11.

12. In the table at the right, as the values in Column 1 increase by 1, the values in Column 2 increase by 5. Fill in the table.

12.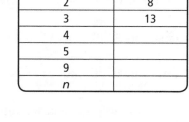

Column 1	Column 2
1	3
2	8
3	13
4	
5	
9	
n	

13. You can cut congruent squares from the corners of a 10 inch-by-10 inch sheet of cardboard and then fold up the sides to form an open box. If the small, cut-out squares have a side length of x, then the formula for the volume V of the box is $V = x \cdot (10 - 2x)^2$. What is the volume if the small squares have 3-inch sides?

13. _____

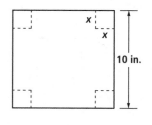
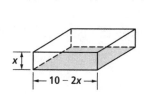

14. Graph the solutions of $w \geq -2$ on the number line.

14. [number line ranging from -5 to 5, labeled w]

15. Graph the solutions of $-4 < x \leq 0$ on the number line.

15. [number line ranging from -5 to 5, labeled x]

16. Convert 3.5^5 to a decimal.

16. _____

17. Write 16.8 billion as a decimal.

17. _____

18. Write 0.0000432 in scientific notation.

18. _____

19. Write 738.3×10^4 in scientific notation.

19. _____

20. Write $10.9 \times \frac{1}{10,000}$ in decimal form.

20. _____

21. Write $4,033 \times 10^0$ in decimal form.

21. _____

22. Evaluate the expression, showing each step in the order of operations.

$16 + 7 \times 10 \div (4^2 - 11)$

22. _____

Chapter 2 Test Cumulative Form

23. Using the numbers 5, −12, and −5, write a correct double
inequality that uses the symbol > two times.

23. _____

24. Show that 4.07 is a rational number by writing it as the ratio
of two integers.

24. _____

**In 25 and 26, tell whether the underlined number is a rate, an
identification, a comparison, or a count.**

25. Mr. Chang lives at <u>557</u> Magnolia Lane.

25. _____

26. The caterer charged $<u>45</u> per person for the reception.

26. _____

27. In which quadrant of the coordinate grid is the point (−7, 7)?

27. _____

28. Give the ordered pair for a point in Quadrant IV.

28. _____

**In 29 and 30, use this scatter plot, which shows the average cost of
tuition and fees at private four-year colleges from 1969 through 2002.
(Note: A year indicates the start of a school year. For example, 1995 is
the 1995–1996 school year.)**

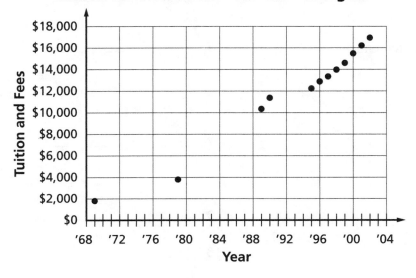

Tuition for U.S. Private Four-Year Colleges

29. What was the average cost for tuition and fees in 1969?

29. _____

30. In which year represented on the graph did the average
tuition cost first exceed $12,000?

30. _____

Quiz Lessons 3-1 through 3-3

In 1 and 2, order the numbers from least to greatest.

1. 0.333, 0.038, 0.0401, 0.340

    1. _____

2. 5.003, 5.00301, 5.00294, 5.00289

    2. _____

3. The following are scores from the men's vault final at the 2004 Olympics:

    Sapronenko: 9.706   Shewfelt: 9.599

    Dragulescu: 9.612   Deferr: 9.737

    a. Order the scores from lowest to highest.

    3. a. _____

    b. Who won the event?

    b. _____

4. Explain how you know that $\frac{984}{616} = \frac{123}{77}$.

    4. _____

    _____

5. Name two numbers that lie between A and B on this number line.

    5. _____

    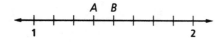

6. Write $<$, $>$, or $=$ to make a true statement.
    $\frac{22}{7}$ _____?_____ $\frac{23}{8}$

    6. _____

In 7–10, find the sum or difference.

7. $\frac{153}{7} + \frac{146}{7}$

    7. _____

8. $\frac{3}{5} + \frac{7}{6}$

    8. _____

9. $\frac{2}{3} + 10\frac{11}{12}$

    9. _____

10. $6\frac{1}{9} - 2\frac{8}{15}$

    10. _____

11. Kendra grew $2\frac{3}{4}$ inches in grade 6, $1\frac{7}{8}$ inches in grade 7, and $2\frac{1}{2}$ inches in grade 8. What total number of inches did she grow in those three grades?

    11. _____

Quiz Lessons 3-4 through 3-6

1. One source gives the airplane distance from the New York to Los Angeles as 2,440 miles. Is this an estimate or an exact measurement? Justify your answer.

   1. _____

   _____

2. Write 3.6717717717... using raised-bar notation.

   2. _____

3. There are 2.54 centimeters in one inch. Estimate the number of centimeters in 2 inches to the nearest centimeter.

   3. _____

4. Use the Substitution Principle to write $\frac{1}{5} + \frac{3}{4}$ as a sum of percents.

   4. _____

5. **Multiple Choice** Which of the following is *not* a name for two fifths?

   5. _____

   A 0.4   B 40%

   C $\frac{6}{15}$ D $2 + \frac{1}{5}$

6. **True or False** $\frac{3}{8} > 50\%$.

   6. _____

7. The Mackenzies ordered dinner from a Thai restaurant. The boys shared pad thai. Pat ate $\frac{1}{3}$ of the dish, Mike ate 33%, and Neal ate 0.3. Who ate the most pad thai? Explain your answer.

   7. _____

8. Round 8765.432 down to the preceding thousand.

   8. _____

9. Write $78.\overline{3}\%$ as a fraction in lowest terms.

   9. _____

10. Write $\frac{7.6}{30.4}$ as a percent.

   10. _____

Name _____

1. **Multiple Choice** Which number is between −0.49 and 0.01 on a number line?

   A −0.51   B 0.1

   C −0.01   D 0.05

1. _____

Below are the first four lines of Alfred Tennyson's 1854 poem *The Charge of the Light Brigade*, which describes a battle during the Crimean War. Use this text in 2–4.

   Half a league, half a league
   Half a league onward
   All in the valley of Death
   Rode the six hundred.

2. According to the poem, what total number of leagues did the six hundred ride?

2. _____

3. Although Tennyson's poem refers to "the six hundred," 673 men took part in the charge. Did Tennyson round up, down, or to the nearest hundred?

3. _____

4. Of the 673 men who took part in the charge, it is estimated that 555 survived the battle.

   a. What fraction of the men is this?

   4. a. _____

   b. What percent of the men is this? Give your answer to the nearest tenth of a percent.

   b. _____

In 5 and 6, write the number as a decimal.

5. $\frac{25}{16}$

5. _____

6. $16\frac{5}{12}$

6. _____

7. a. Evaluate $\frac{4}{5} - \frac{6}{11}$ and write the difference as a fraction in lowest terms.

   7. a. _____

   b. Express the difference as a decimal.

   b. _____

   c. In your answer to Part b, what digit is in the millionths place?

   c. _____

Chapter 3 Test Form A

8. Write <, =, or > to make a true statement.

    a. 65.201 ___?___ $65.\overline{20}$

    b. $\frac{9.36}{11.5}$ ___?___ $\frac{9}{11}$

    c. $-3.\overline{39}$ ___?___ $-3\frac{13}{33}$

9. a. What is the distance between consecutive tick marks on this number line?

    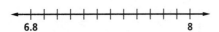
    6.8   8

    b. Graph the values 7.15 and 7.88 on the number line above.

10. Write $16.\overline{6}\%$ as a fraction in lowest terms.

11. Write 6.3% as a decimal.

12. If 20 comic books cost $57.95, estimate the cost of one comic book.

13. Suppose a regular six-sided die is rolled. What is the probability that the result is either 1 or greater than 4?

14. A school-supply store sells plastic rulers in groups of 144 for $45.

    a. If the store priced individual rulers at the same rate, how much would it charge for one ruler?

    b. A group of 144 items is called a *gross*. If a school needs 300 rulers, how many gross should it buy?

15. Carlos's restaurant check is for $24.50. If he wants to add a 17% tip, what total amount should he pay?

16. Estimate $\sqrt{43}$ to the nearest thousandth.

17. Does $5\frac{2}{3} = \frac{34}{6}$? Justify your answer.

8. a. _____

   b. _____

   c. _____

9. a. _____

10. _____

11. _____

12. _____

13. _____

14. a. _____

    b. _____

15. _____

16. _____

17. _____

Chapter 3 Test Form A

18. Write 4.9234343434... using the raised-bar symbol.

18. _____

19. Rewrite $0.34 + 0.17$ as a sum of percents.

19. _____

20. Suppose a square table has an area of 49 square feet.

a. What is the length of one side?

20. a. _____

b. Estimate the length of the diagonal of the table to the nearest tenth of a foot.

b. _____

21. If 12 states are considered to be in the "Midwest" of the United States, what is the probability that a state picked at random will be in the Midwest? Write your answer as a percent.

21. _____

22. Evaluate $\frac{45}{66} + \frac{7}{12}$.

22. _____

Chapter 3 Test Form B

1. **Multiple Choice** Which number is between −0.39 and 0.001 on a number line?

   A −0.40   B −0.01

   C 0.0011   D 10^{-2}

1. _____

Below are the first four lines of Alfred Tennyson's 1854 poem *The Charge of the Light Brigade*, which describes a battle during the Crimean War. Use this text in 2–4.

> *Half a league, half a league*
> *Half a league onward*
> *All in the valley of Death*
> *Rode the six hundred.*

2. Although Tennyson's poem refers to "the six hundred," 673 men took part in the charge. Did Tennyson round up, down, or to the nearest hundred?

2. _____

3. Of the 673 men who took part in the charge, 118 died in the battle.

   a. What fraction of the men is this?

   3. a. _____

   b. What percent of the men is this? Give your answer to the nearest tenth of a percent.

   b. _____

4. According to the poem, what total number of leagues did the six hundred ride?

4. _____

In 5 and 6, write the number as a decimal.

5. $\frac{33}{16}$

5. _____

6. $9\frac{7}{11}$

6. _____

7. a. Evaluate $\frac{3}{5} - \frac{4}{11}$ and write the difference as a fraction in lowest terms.

   7. a. _____

   b. Express the difference as a decimal.

   b. _____

   c. In your answer to Part b, what digit is in the millionths place?

   c. _____

8. Write $<$, $=$, or $>$ to make a true statement.

   a. $-7.\overline{78}$ ____?____ $-7\frac{26}{33}$

   b. $\frac{7.29}{11.4}$ ____?____ $\frac{7}{11}$

   c. 49.322 ____?____ $49.\overline{32}$

8. a. _____

   b. _____

   c. _____

9. a. What is the distance between consecutive tick marks on this number line?

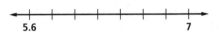

   b. Graph the values 5.9 and 6.45 on the number line above.

9. a. _____

10. Write $83.\overline{3}\%$ as a fraction in lowest terms.

10. _____

11. Write 4.9% as a decimal.

11. _____

12. If 30 mangoes cost \$35.70, estimate the cost of one mango.

12. _____

13. Suppose a regular six-sided die is rolled. What is the probability that the result is either 6 or less than or equal to 3?

13. _____

14. A computer store sells CDs in packs of 72 for \$42.

   a. If the store priced individual CDs at the same rate, how much would it charge for one CD?

   b. If a company needs 600 CDs, how many packs should it buy?

14. a. _____

   b. _____

15. Carlos wants to buy a shirt that costs \$29.80. The sales tax is 6%. What total amount will Carlos have to pay for the shirt?

15. _____

16. Estimate $\sqrt{67}$ to the nearest thousandth.

16. _____

17. Does $2\frac{3}{8} = \frac{57}{24}$? Justify your answer.

17. _____

Chapter 3 Test   Form B

18. Write 1.48382382382. . . using the raised-bar symbol.

18. _____

19. Rewrite $0.07 + 0.81$ as a sum of percents.

19. _____

20. Suppose a square carpet has an area of 36 square feet.

    a. What is the length of one side?

20. a. _____

    b. Estimate the length of the diagonal of the carpet to the nearest tenth of a foot.

    b. _____

21. If 9 states are considered to be in the "Northeast" of the United States, what is the probability that a state picked at random will be in the Northeast? Write your answer as a percent.

21. _____

22. Evaluate $\frac{32}{56} + \frac{11}{21}$.

22. _____

Chapter 3 Test Form C

1. Explain why the decimals 0.24, $0.2\overline{4}$, and $0.\overline{24}$ are not equal to each other. Then use these three decimals to fill in the blanks below.

   _____ > _____ > _____

2. Tasha ate $\frac{1}{4}$ of a sausage pizza. Ollie ate $\frac{3}{8}$ of a same-size mushroom pizza. What fraction of a whole pizza did they eat in all? Make drawings to explain your solution.

3. Describe a situation in which it is appropriate to round a decimal up and a situation in which it is appropriate to round a decimal down. Give specific examples to show how you would round the decimals involved.

4. Explain why each step shown below is true.

   Step 1: $5\frac{1}{4}\% = 5.25\%$

   Step 2: $= 5.25 \times 0.01$

   Step 3: $= 0.0525$

5. Suppose the price of an item is increased by 10%. Then, the new price is decreased by 10%. Is the final price equal to the original price? Does it matter what the original price is? Explain your answers.

6. Squares with *areas* 10, 20, 30, 40, and 50 are drawn on separate slips of paper. One square is chosen at random. What is the probability that a *side length* of the square is greater than 5? Show your work.

   Write and solve your own probability question about the side lengths of the squares.

Chapter 3 Test Form D

The Student Government at Midfield Middle School plans to sponsor an after-school event in the spring. Each grade was asked to collect data on the type of event students would prefer and to make a circle graph of the results. The grades produced the three graphs shown at the right. As you can see, the first graph is labeled with whole numbers, the second is labeled with fractions, and the third is labeled with percents.

As the secretary of the Student Government, it is your job to adjust the graphs and summarize the data.

a. What kinds of numbers do you think should be used to label the graphs: percents, fractions, or whole-number counts? Explain your reasoning.

b. Trace the outlines of the three graphs onto a separate sheet of paper, but do *not* copy the labels. Using the method that you chose in Part a, adjust the graphs so that all three are labeled in the same way.

c. Use the data from the graphs. What total number of students would prefer a concert? What fraction of all students is this? What percent?

d. Make a table that shows the *combined* data for all three grades.

e. A *trend* is a pattern of change in data. The Student Government president has asked if you see any trends in these data from grade to grade. Write a brief report to answer the president's question.

Grade 6 (300 students)

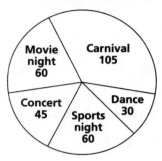

Grade 7 (360 students)

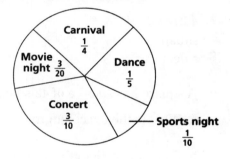

Grade 8 (240 students)

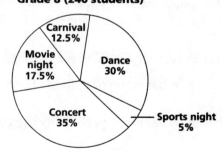

Chapter 3 Test Cumulative Form

In 1–4, find the sum or difference.

1. $3\frac{2}{3} + 1\frac{5}{12}$

2. $\frac{6}{7} - \frac{2}{5}$

3. $\frac{2}{7} + \frac{5}{8} + \frac{1}{4}$

4. $2\frac{5}{9} - 1\frac{2}{3}$

1. _____

2. _____

3. _____

4. _____

In 5–8, order the numbers from least to greatest.

5. $-0.078, -0.78, -0.0078$

6. $\frac{4}{11}, \frac{1}{3}, \frac{5}{13}$

7. $4.2\overline{7}, 4.27, 4.\overline{27}$

8. $-\frac{7}{12}, -\frac{1}{2}, -\frac{5}{9}$

5. _____

6. _____

7. _____

8. _____

9. A square has an area of 42 square units.

   a. What is the exact length of one side?

   b. Estimate the length of a side to the nearest hundredth.

9. **a.** _____

   b. _____

10. Suppose sales tax is 7%. How much would you pay in sales tax for a pair of jeans priced at $39.75?

10. _____

11. A regular six-sided die is rolled.

    a. What is the probability the result is less than 5?

    b. What is the probability the result is greater than 6?

11. **a.** _____

    b. _____

12. What numbers do the points represent?

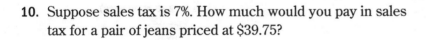

12. **a.** _____

    b. _____

Chapter 3 Test Cumulative Form

13. Write a simple fraction equal to 3.409.

13. _____

14. Write 0.009 as a percent.

14. _____

15. **a.** Round 32.768 to the nearest tenth.

15. **a.** _____

   b. Round 32.768 to the preceding half.

   b. _____

16. **a.** Plot and label points *A–D* on coordinate grid at right.

   $A = (-8, 2)$ $B = (1, -4)$ $C = (-6, -6)$ $D = (3, 7)$

16. **a.**

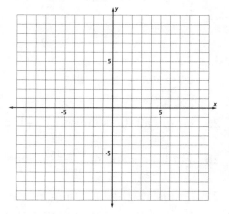

   b. In which quadrant is point *A*?

   b. _____

In 17 and 18, write the number in scientific notation.

17. 636.4×10^{-9}

17. _____

18. 45,565,900

18. _____

19. Evaluate the expression below, showing each step in the order of operations.

   $(14 - 6)^2 + 27 \div 3$

19. _____

In 20 and 21, identify the underlined number as a rate or a ratio. If it is a rate, tell what two units are being compared.

20. Mario can type <u>65</u> words per minute.

20. _____

21. This year <u>1.5</u> times as many people attended the school play as last year.

21. _____

22. Write the following numbers in order from least to greatest: $-3, 0, -7, 3$.

22. _____

23. Find the value of *w* in the drawing below.

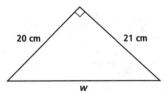

23. _____

24. Three instances of a pattern are given. Describe the general pattern using three variables.

$$\frac{2 + 5}{3} = \frac{2}{3} + \frac{5}{3}$$

$$\frac{-11 + 4}{7} = \frac{-11}{7} + \frac{4}{7}$$

$$\frac{2.2 + 19.7}{23} = \frac{2.2}{23} + \frac{19.7}{23}$$

24. _____

25. Graph all the solutions of $-1 < x \le 3.5$.

25.

26. Find the value of $\frac{c^2 - 3ab}{(a + c)^2}$ when $a = 2$, $b = 3$, and $c = 5$.

26. _____

27. Translate the following into an algebraic expression: 7 times the square of the sum of a number and 12.

27. _____

28. In the table at right, the numbers in Column 2 increase by 3 for every increase of 1 in the Column 1 numbers. Complete the table.

28.

Column 1	Column 2
1	5
2	8
3	a.
4	b.
5	c.
100	d.
n	e.

29. Find the solution of $87 - x = 75$.

29. _____

30. Give two solutions of $r - 10 < 6$.

30. _____

Comprehensive Test Chapters 1–3

1. $6^4 = $ _____?_____   1. _____

   A 24   B 10
   C 216   D 1,296

2. $0.39 \times 10^{-5} = $ _____?_____   2. _____

   A 0.000039   B 390,000
   C 0.0000039   D 3,900,000

3. 19.6 billion is _____?_____ .   3. _____

   A 19.600,000,000   B 19,600,000
   C 1,960,000,000   D 19,600,000,000

4. Which number is written in scientific notation?   4. _____

   A 72×10^4 B 7.2×10^4
   C 7.2×8^3 D $7.2 \times 10^{3.5}$

5. $15 - 3 \cdot 2 + 1 = $ _____?_____   5. _____

   A 10   B 36
   C 25   D 6

6. Which of the following is *not* a rational number?   6. _____

   A $5.\overline{68}$ B 16π
   C $\frac{4.37}{11.1566}$ D $\frac{0}{3}$

7. Which of the following is *not* equal to $417.4 \times \frac{1}{10,000}$?   7. _____

   A 0.04174   B 4.174×10^{-2}
   C $41.74 \times \frac{1}{1,000}$ D $41.74 \times \frac{1}{10^4}$

8. In which statement is 7 being used as a measure?   8. _____

   A A week is 7 times longer than a day.
   B Mali earns \$7 per hour working at the park.
   C There are 7 clownfish in the tank.
   D The glass contains 7 ounces of water.

Name _____

9. Three less than the square of a number can be written as ____?____ .

    A $3 - n^2$ B $3 < n^2$
    C $n^2 - 3$ D $2n - 3$

9. _____

10. Which inequality does this graph represent?

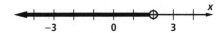

    A $x < 2$ B $x \leq 2$
    C $x > 2$ D $x \geq 2$

10. _____

11. Which of the following is a Pythagorean triple?

    A 12, 15, 20 B 20, 48, 52
    C 17, 24, 30 D 6, 11, 12

11. _____

12. Which of the following is a solution of $3x - 7 = 17$?

    A $3\frac{1}{3}$ B 8
    C 10 D 24

12. _____

13. Which of the following is a solution of $4x - 2 > 10$?

    A 1 B 2
    C 3 D 4

13. _____

14. Below are three instances of a pattern. Which expression describes the general pattern?

    $$5 \div \tfrac{1}{2} = 5 \cdot 2$$
    $$37.7 \div \tfrac{1}{2} = 37.7 \cdot 2$$
    $$-14 \div \tfrac{1}{2} = -14 \cdot 2$$

    A $x \div \tfrac{1}{2} = x \cdot 2$ B $5 \div \tfrac{1}{n} = 5 \cdot n$
    C $a \div m = a \cdot n$ D $a \div \tfrac{1}{m} = a \cdot n$

14. _____

15. For a small dog over two years of age, the formula $h = 24 + 4(d - 2)$ can be used to convert the dog's age d to the equivalent age in human years. Sandra's Chihuahua is 9 years old. How old is this in "human years"?

    A 52 years B 60 years
    C 63 years D 196 years

15. _____

Comprehensive Test   Chapters 1–3

16. A right triangle has legs with lengths 5 units and 7 units. What is the length of the hypotenuse?

   A $\sqrt{13}$ units   **B** $\sqrt{24}$ units

   C $\sqrt{74}$ units   **D** 74 units

16. _____

17. Which decimal is equal to four thousandths?

   A 4,000   **B** 0.4000

   C 0.004   **D** 0.0004

17. _____

18. Two thirds, as a decimal rounded to the nearest hundredth, is _____?_____.

   A 0.23   **B** 0.66

   C 0.666   **D** 0.67

18. _____

19. Which number is graphed on the number line?

   A $2\frac{1}{4}$ **B** -1.75

   C -2.25 **D** -2.4

19. _____

20. Which symbol makes this statement true: $\frac{2}{3}$ _____?_____ $\frac{3}{4}$?

   A $>$ **B** $<$

   C $=$ **D** $\geq$

20. _____

21. Which number is *not* equal to the other three?

   A $\frac{3}{11}$ **B** 0.27

   C $0.\overline{27}$ **D** $0.27\overline{2}$

21. _____

22. $\frac{5}{9} - \frac{1}{4} =$ _____?_____

   A $\frac{11}{36}$ **B** $\frac{4}{5}$

   C $\frac{6}{13}$ **D** $\frac{29}{36}$

22. _____

23. Which is the length of a side of a square with an area of 10 square units?

   A 2.5 units   **B** $\sqrt{10}$ units

   C 40 units   **D** 100 units

23. _____

Comprehensive Test Chapters 1–3

24. As a fraction in lowest terms, $80\% =$ _____?_____.

    A $\frac{80}{100}$

    B $\frac{8}{10}$

    C $\frac{4}{5}$

    D 0.8

24. _____

25. If a marble is drawn at random from a bag containing 3 red marbles, 4 blue marbles, and 1 yellow marble, what is the probability the marble is *not* red?

    A $\frac{3}{8}$

    B $\frac{3}{5}$

    C $\frac{5}{8}$

    D 5

25. _____

26. Which double inequality is correct?

    A $-7 < 3 > -2$

    B $-2 > -7 < 3$

    C $3 > -2 > -7$

    D $3 < -2 < -7$

26. _____

27. $4 + \frac{5}{6} =$ _____?_____.

    A $\frac{24}{6}$

    B $\frac{29}{6}$

    C $\frac{20}{6}$

    D $\frac{45}{6}$

27. _____

28. Which spreadsheet formula computes half of the sum of the values in cells C6 and C7?

    A $=0.5*C6+C7$

    B $=0.5+C6+C7$

    C $=0.5*C6*C7$

    D $=0.5*(C6+C7)$

28. _____

29. 125% of 48 = _____?_____.

    A 6

    B 12

    C 60

    D 6,000

29. _____

30. Which point is in quadrant III on the coordinate grid?

    A $(0, -5)$

    B $(-9, -1)$

    C $(3, -8)$

    D $(-4, 3)$

30. _____

31. Which number is *not* equal to the other three?

    A 0.125

    B 12.5%

    C $\frac{1}{8}$

    D $\frac{12}{5}$

31. _____

32. When $c = 7$ and $b = 3$, then $c^b =$ _____?_____.

    A 21

    B 73

    C 343

    D 2,187

32. _____

Quiz Lessons 4-1 through 4-3

1. Tell whether the following statement is true or false. If it is false, give a counterexample.

   All multiples of 40 are multiples of 80.

   1. _____

In 2 and 3, fill in the blank with *always, sometimes but not always*, or *never* to form a true statement.

2. If you add zero to any number, you ____?____ change the value of the number.

   2. _____

3. A parallelogram is ____?____ a rhombus.

   3. _____

4. Write a true if-then statement using this Venn diagram.

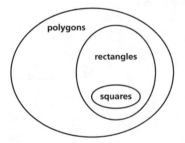

5. Your friend says, "I didn't see nothing." Apply the Op-Op property to write an equivalent statement.

   5. _____

6. **Multiple Choice** Which number is the additive inverse of *n*?

   6. _____

   A 1   **B** 0   **C** $\frac{1}{n}$ **D** $-n$

7. Find the value of the variable that makes this equation true.

   7. _____

   $-(-(-(-(-(-h))))) = -1.9$

8. Consider the following statement.

   You will be in trouble if you hit your little brother.

   a. Write the hypothesis.   8. a. _____

   b. Write the conclusion.   b. _____

   c. Write the converse.   c. _____

Quiz Lessons 4-4 through 4-6

1. Let $M = \{0, 2, 4, 6, 8\}$ and $N = \{2, 3, 5, 7\}$.

   a. Find $M \cap N$.

   b. Find $M \cup N$.

   1. a. _____

   b. _____

In 2 and 3, graph the solutions and describe the solution set geometrically.

2. $w \leq -9.8$ or $w \geq -6.5$

2. ⊢+++++++++++⊣

3. $q \geq -\frac{5}{4}$ and $q \geq \frac{5}{4}$

3. ⊢+++++++++++⊣

True or False   In 4 and 5, refer to the Venn Diagram. Tell whether each statement is true or false.

4. All students in Algebra Club are using *UCSMP Algebra*.

   Students at Oakdale Middle School

   Students using *Transition Mathematics*

   Students using *UCSMP Algebra*

   Students in Band

   Students in Algebra Club

   4. _____

5. Some students in the band are using *Transition Mathematics*.

   5. _____

6. **True or False**   A square is a union of four segments of equal length in which each segment intersects exactly two others, one at each of its endpoints.

   6. _____

7. Refer to the figure at the right.

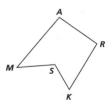

   a. Classify the figure based on the number of sides.

   7. a. _____

   b. Name a vertex.

   b. _____

   c. Name a side.

   c. _____

   d. Give two names for the figure.

   d. _____

Name _____

In 1 and 2, find the value of the variable that makes each equation
true. Then tell what property the equation represents.

1. $0 + 2m = 2(13)$ 1. _____   _____

2. $-(-(-4)) = n$ 2. _____   _____

In 3–6, fill in the blank with *always, sometimes but not always,* or
never to form a true statement.

3. Supplementary angles are ____?____ adjacent.   3. _____

4. A rhombus is ____?____ a rectangle.   4. _____

5. A parallelogram is ____?____ a trapezoid.   5. _____

6. Two angles whose measures have a sum of 90° are   6. _____
   ____?____ complementary.

7. Let M = the set of all monkeys and N = the set of all animals.

   a. Find $M \cap N$.   7. a. _____

   b. Find $M \cup N$.   b. _____

True or False   In 8 and 9, tell whether the statement is true or false.

8. $7.2 \cdot 10^{-4}$ is a negative number.   8. _____

9. The ratio of the circumference of a circle to its diameter is a   9. _____
   rational number.

10. a. Write the converse of the following statement:

    If there is a thunderstorm, then the barbecue will be ruined.

    _____

    b. Is the converse always true?   10. b. _____

11. a. Use the following if-then statement to write a definition
    for *polygon*.

    If a figure is a polygon, then it has sides and angles.

    _____

    b. Is this a good definition? Explain why or why not.   11. b. _____

    _____

Chapter 4 Test   Form A

12. **a.** Graph the set of all numbers x such that $-13 \leq x \leq -8$.

    b. Describe the graph from Part a geometrically.

12. **a.**

    b. _____

13. Graph the set of all numbers p such that $p > 2.5$ or $p \leq -2.5$.

13.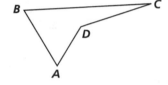

14. Write an inequality based on the number line below.

                                                            q

        2.3   2.4

14. _____

15. **a.** Classify the figure below according to the number of sides it has.

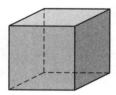

    b. Name its sides.

    c. Give two names for the figure.

15. **a.** _____

    b. _____

    c. _____

16. Give an example of a number that is an integer but not a whole number.

16. _____

17. Explain why the figure below is not a polygon.

    _____

18. Create a Venn diagram showing the relationships among these sets: multiples of 2, multiples of 4, multiples of 7.

18.

Chapter 4 Test Form A

19. Identify the hypothesis and conclusion of the following statement.

    If a polygon has exactly 12 sides, then it is a dodecagon.

19. Hypothesis: _____

    _____

    Conclusion: _____

    _____

20. Sets *A*, *B*, and *C* are described below. Create a Venn diagram showing the relationships among these sets.

    A = television shows that are 30 minutes long

    B = television shows that are 60 minutes long

    C = television shows that are 30 minutes, 60 minutes, 90 minutes, or 2 hours long

20, 21.

21. Refer to Question 20. Suppose *D* is the set of television shows that are 2 hours long. Represent set *D* in the Venn diagram for Question 20.

22. Make a hierarchy of the following sets of numbers: rational numbers, real numbers, whole numbers, irrational numbers, and integers.

22.

23. Give three ways to name the angle below.

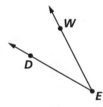

23. _____

24. Consider the following statement.

    All four-legged animals are dogs.

    a. Write the statement in if-then form.

    _____

    b. Give a counterexample that proves the statement is false.

24. b. _____

Chapter 4 Test Form B

In 1 and 2, find the value of the variable that makes each equation true. Then tell what property the equation represents.

1. $p + -0.67 = 0$

1. _____   _____

2. $v + 3\pi = 3\pi$

2. _____   _____

In 3–6, fill in the blank with *always*, *sometimes but not always*, or *never* to form a true statement.

3. A square is __?__ a rhombus.

3. _____

4. An obtuse triangle __?__ has an acute angle.

4. _____

5. An isosceles triangle is __?__ equilateral.

5. _____

6. A diagonal of a polygon is __?__ a side of the polygon.

6. _____

7. Let M = the set of all mammals and F = the set of all fish.

   a. Find $M \cap F$.

   b. Find $M \cup F$.

7. a. _____

   b. _____

True or False In 8 and 9, tell whether the statement is true or false.

8. $2n$ is an even number for any integer value of n.

8. _____

9. The product of two prime numbers is a prime number.

9. _____

10. a. Write the converse of the following statement:

    If you are at a rock concert, then you will hear music.

    _____

    b. Is the converse always true?

10. b. _____

11. a. Use the following if-then statement to write a definition for *parallelogram*.

    If a quadrilateral is a parallelogram, then it has parallel sides.

    _____

    b. Is this a good definition? Explain why or why not.

11. b. _____

    _____

12. **a.** Graph the set of all numbers x such that $-9 \leq x \leq -4$.

    b. Describe the graph from Part a geometrically.

12. **a.**

    b. _____

13. Graph the set of all numbers p such that $p \geq 3$ or $p < -1.5$.

13.

14. Write an inequality based on the number line below.

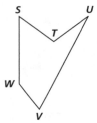

14. _____

15. **a.** Classify the figure below according to the number of sides it has.

15. **a.** _____

    b. Name its sides.

    b. _____

    c. Give two names for the figure.

    c. _____

16. Give an example of a rational number that is not an integer.

16. _____

17. Explain why the figure below is not a polygon.

    _____

18. Create a Venn diagram showing the relationships among these sets: multiples of 3, multiples of 6, multiples of 5.

18.

Chapter 4 Test   Form B

19. Identify the hypothesis and conclusion of the following statement.

    If a quadrilateral has four right angles, then it is a rectangle.

19. Hypothesis: _____

    _____

    Conclusion: _____

    _____

20. Sets A, B, and C are described below. Create a Venn diagram showing the relationships among these sets.

    A = people who have cats as pets

    B = people who have dogs as pets

    C = people who have cats, dogs, fish, or birds as pets

20, 21.

21. Refer to Question 20. Suppose D is the set of people who have birds as pets. Represent set D in the Venn diagram for Question 20.

22. Make a hierarchy of the following sets of numbers: rational numbers, real numbers, whole numbers, irrational numbers, and integers.

22.

23. Give three possible names for the angle below.

23. _____

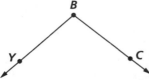

24. Consider the following statement:

    All vegetables are green.

    a. Write the statement in if-then form.

    _____

    b. Give a counterexample that proves the statement is false.

24. b. _____

Name _____

Chapter 4 Test   Form C

1. Complete this statement so that *both* the statement *and* its converse are true. Give the converse statement.

   If a number is odd, then

   _____

   Complete the statement so that the statement is true, but its converse is false. Give the converse statement.

   If a number is odd, then

   _____

2. Give two inequalities so that the *intersection* of their solution sets on the number line is

   a. a point. _____

   b. a ray. _____

   c. a segment. _____

   d. the empty set. _____

   Give two inequalities so that the *union* of their solution sets on the number line is

   e. a line. _____

   f. a ray. _____

3. Connect the points on the left to form a polygon. Name the polygon, and classify it according to the number of sides it has.

   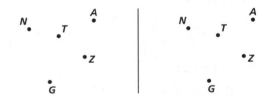

   Connect points on the right to form a figure that is not a polygon. Explain why the figure does not fit the definition of *polygon*.

4. This hierarchy shows some items sold in a clothing store. Make a hierarchy for a different type of store (for example, sporting goods, music, grocery, furniture). Your hierarchy should have at least six terms and at least three levels.

   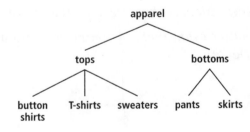

Copyright © Wright Group/McGraw-Hill

49

Chapter 4 Test Form D

There are several possible definitions for parallelogram, rectangle, rhombus, and square. Below, we give the definition presented in your book and an alternative definition for each of these quadrilaterals.

Choose at least three of the quadrilaterals. Do the following for each:

- Write the alternative definition as an if-then statement, and then write its converse.

- Using drawings and logical reasoning, present convincing evidence that both the statement and its converse *appear to be* true. (You will learn how to *prove* that the statements are true when you take a geometry course.)

Parallelogram

Book definition: A parallelogram is a quadrilateral with two pairs of parallel sides.

Alternative definition: A parallelogram is a quadrilateral whose diagonals divide each other in half.

Rectangle

Book definition: A rectangle is a parallelogram with four right angles.

Alternative definition: A rectangle is a parallelogram with a right angle.

Rhombus

Book definition: A rhombus is a parallelogram with all sides the same length.

Alternative definition: A rhombus is a parallelogram in which two of the touching (adjacent) sides are the same length.

Square

Book definition: A square is a rectangle with all sides the same length.

Alternative definition: A square is a rhombus with diagonals that are the same length.

Chapter 4 Test Cumulative Form

1. Let A be the set of factors of 36. Let B be the set of factors of 27.

    a. Find $A \cup B$.

    b. Find $A \cap B$.

2. Draw an obtuse angle CUB.

1. a. _____

   b. _____

2.

In 3 and 4, fill in the blank with *always, sometimes but not always*, or *never* to form a true statement.

3. A natural number is ____?____ an integer.

4. A rhombus ____?____ a square.

5. The equation below is an instance of what property?

    $34.9 + 0 = 34.9$

6. What property states that $-(-x) = x$?

7. Consider to the following true statement:

    If an animal is a horse, then it has hooves.

    a. What is the hypothesis of the statement?

    _____

    b. What is the conclusion?

    _____

    c. Write the converse of the statement.

    _____

    d. Is the converse true? If not, give a counterexample.

3. _____

4. _____

5. _____

6. _____

7. d. _____

8. Draw a figure that is the union of four segments but is *not* a quadrilateral.

8.

9. For the definition below, write a true if-then statement and its true converse.

The greatest common factor *of two numbers is the greatest whole number that is a factor of both numbers.*

_____

_____

10. Give an example of a negative irrational number.

10. _____

11. Give an example of an odd positive integer.

11. _____

12. Graph the set of all numbers x such that $x \geq -2$ or $x < -5$.

12. ┼─┼─┼─┼─┼─┼─┼─┼─┼─►

13. Graph the set of all numbers x such that $x \leq 4$ and $x > -1$.

13. ┼─┼─┼─┼─┼─┼─┼─┼─┼─►

14. Add the sets *miniature poodles* and *hamsters* to the hierarchy at the right.

14.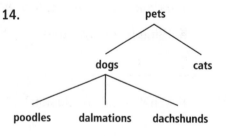

15. Add the set of multiples of 15 to the Venn diagram at right.

15.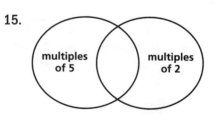

16. Write the number 0.0000047 in scientific notation.

16. _____

17. Write 18.7 trillion as a decimal.

17. _____

18. In which quadrant on a coordinate grid is the point $(-7, 13)$?

18. _____

19. Evaluate $\dfrac{14 + 2 \times 3 - 3^2}{5 + \sqrt{9 \cdot 4}}$.

19. _____

20. Write 833.7×10^{12} in scientific notation.

20. _____

21. Give two solutions of $2x < 10$.

21. _____

22. Translate the following into an algebraic expression: a number times eleven, then the product increased by 5.

22. _____

23. **True or False** The numbers 45, 28, and 53 are a Pythagorean triple.

23. _____

24. The formula $A = \frac{1}{2}h(b + B)$ relates the area A of a trapezoid to its height h and the lengths of the two bases b and B. Find the area of a trapezoid with height 5 centimeters and bases of length 3 centimeters and 7 centimeters.

24. _____

25. Three instances of a pattern are given. Describe the general pattern using variables.

With tax, a $12 item costs $12 + 0.06 × $12.

With tax, a $64 item costs $64 + 0.06 × $64.

With tax, a $2.25 item costs $2.25 + 0.06 × $2.25.

25. _____

26. Write three million, seven hundred two thousand and two thousandths as a decimal.

26. _____

27. Add: $1\frac{5}{8} + 3\frac{11}{14}$.

27. _____

28. Write $\frac{5}{6}$ as a decimal and as a percent.

28. _____

29. A square has an area of 54 square centimeters. Find the exact length of one side of the square.

29. _____

30. A bag contains 7 black marbles, 12 green marbles, 4 purple marbles, and 2 red marbles. If one marble is selected at random, what is the probability that it is purple or red?

30. _____

Quiz Lessons 5-1 through 5-4

In 1-4, simplify.

1. $59 + (-67)$

2. $-1.5 - 2.5$

3. $a + 3 + (-a) - (-3)$

4. $\left|-\frac{1}{5}\right| - \left(\left|\frac{1}{5}\right|\right)$

5. Consider the addition $4 + (-5) = -1$.

   a. Picture the addition on a number line

   b. Represent the addition in a fact triangle.

1. _____

2. _____

3. _____

4. _____

5. a.

   b.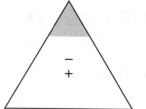

6. A clockwise turn of 70° followed by a counterclockwise turn of 50° is the same as a counterclockwise turn of 50° followed by a clockwise turn of 70°. What property of addition justifies this statement?

6. _____

7. A recipe calls for b cups of broccoli, c cups of chopped onions, and d cups of diced celery, for a total of v cups of vegetables. Write an equation relating b, c, d, and v.

7. _____

8. A movie made $28 million in its first week at the box office, but only $6 million in its second week. How much more money did it make the first week than the second week?

8. _____

9. The temperature of a pot of water boiling at 100°C is brought down to T degrees Celsius. Write an expression for the decrease in temperature.

9. _____

10. Rewrite the expression $a - b$, using the algebraic definition of subtraction.

10. _____

Quiz **Lessons 5-5 through 5-8**

In 1–4, solve.

1. $r - 8 = -5$

1. _____

2. $\frac{3}{2} + x = 2$

2. _____

In 3 and 4, solve the inequality and then graph all the solutions.

3. $t + (-4) \leq 88$

3. <!-- number line --> ⟵+++++++++++⟶

4. $\frac{4}{5} > -\frac{2}{5} + p$

4. <!-- number line --> ⟵+++++++++++⟶

5. What property can be used to show that if
   $x + 12.8 = -1.6$, then $x + 12.8 + -12.8 = -1.6 + -12.8$?

5. _____

6. Graph the line with equation $x + y = -1$.

6.
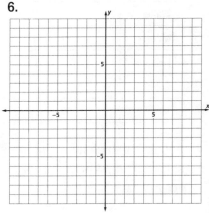

7. Suppose you roll two fair six-sided dice. What is the
   probability of rolling

   a. doubles?

   7. a. _____

   b. two odd numbers?

   b. _____

   c. both doubles and two odd numbers?

   c. _____

   d. doubles or two odd numbers?

   d. _____

8. Consider this problem: Dan's best time in the 100-meter
   dash is 14.4 seconds. The school record is 13.72 seconds.
   How much longer is his time than the school record?

   a. Write an addition equation to represent this problem.

   8. a. _____

   b. Solve your equation.

   b. _____

Name _____

You will need a calculator, a compass, and a straightedge for this test.

In 1–3, calculate.

1. $0 - 3.75 - (5 - 1\frac{1}{2})$

2. $(-23 + \frac{17}{15}) + (23 + -\frac{17}{15}) + (5 + 9 + -5)$

3. $|-14 + -0.8| - |-3.2| + |-1.6|$

1. _____

2. _____

3. _____

In 4 and 5, use the table below, which gives information about six men auditioning for the lead role in a play.

Name	Height (inches)	Hair Color
Jerome	67	Red
Walter	75	Black
Miles	65.5	Blonde
Leshaun	72	Black
Colin	80	Red
Jamie	64	Brown

4. Assuming each actor has an equal probability of being selected, what is the probability that the role will go to an actor with black hair?

4. _____

5. What is the probability the role will go to an actor at least 5 feet 9 inches tall who does not have black hair?

5. _____

6. On October 19, 1987, the Dow Jones Industrial Average fell 508.00 points to 1738.74. What was the average at the start of the day?

6. _____

7. **Multiple Choice** Which equation is represented by the graph below?

7. _____

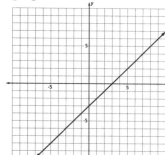

A $y = -x + 3$ **B** $y = -x + -3$

C $y - x = 3$ **D** $y - x = -3$

8. Consider this problem: Blaise bought a used car for $3,250. He added a turbocharger that cost *t* dollars and a new air intake that cost $178, bringing the total cost to $3,587. How much did the turbocharger cost?

   a. Write an equation to represent this problem.   8. a. _____

   b. Solve your equation.   b. _____

9. **Multiple Choice** Which of the following is a solution of   9. _____
   $x + -3.4 > \frac{17}{68}$?

   A 3.4   B 0

   C $\frac{21}{68}$ D 4.25

10. The bicycle below is moving right to left. The fork of the   10. _____
    bicycle attaches to the front wheel at an angle of 35° with
    the vertical line. *F* is the point on the wheel at the fork.
    When the bike moves forward, how many degrees does
    F need to rotate before it touches the ground?

11. a. What addition is represented on the number line below?   11. a. _____

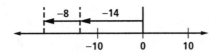

    b. What is the sum?   b. _____

12. Construct a triangle with the following side lengths: 12.

    _____ *a*

    _____ *b*

    _____ *c*

13. Simplify the expression $a + b + (-b) - (-a)$.   13. _____

14. **Multiple Choice** Which property justifies the following   14. _____
    statement: If $w + -8 = 16$, then $w + -8 + 8 = 16 + 8$?

    A Commutative Property of Addition

    B Associative Property of Addition

    C Addition Property of Equality

    D Addition Property of Zero

In 15–17, consider the equation $9.35 + x = 1.89$.

15. Draw the fact triangle that represents this equation.   15.

16. Use the fact triangle to write two facts related to the original   16. _____
    equation.

    _____

17. Solve the equation for x.   17. _____

18. On Monday, the water level of a lake dropped 3 inches from   18. _____
    its level on Sunday. On Tuesday, it fell another 2.5 inches.
    On Wednesday, it rained, and the level rose by 1 foot. On
    Thursday, it fell $1\frac{1}{2}$ inches. What was the change in the level
    of the lake from Sunday to Thursday?

19. Can a triangle have side lengths 19 miles, 10 miles, and   19. _____
    8 miles? Justify your answer.

20. José lives 2.8 miles from Sheila and 1.6 miles from Perry.

    a. Write a double inequality to represent the possible   20. a. _____
       distances d between Sheila's home and Perry's home.

    b. Graph the inequality on the number line.   b. ‹—+—+—+—+—+—+—+—+—+—+—›

Chapter 5 Test Form B

You will need a calculator, a compass, and a straightedge for this test.

In 1–3, calculate.

1. $0 - 6.25 - (-3 + 2\frac{3}{4})$

    1. _____

2. $(-11 - 4 + 11) - (-19 - \frac{4}{13}) + (19 + \frac{4}{13})$

    2. _____

3. $|-1.3| + |11.5| - |-5.7 - -8.9|$

    3. _____

In 4 and 5, use the table below, which gives information about eight girls on a basketball team.

Name	Jersey Number	Position
Jing	11	Forward
Tamika	23	Guard
Kate	8	Forward
Shaundra	34	Center
Erin	2	Guard
Jamie	17	Guard
Tia	22	Forward
Luisa	13	Center

4. The coach will select the team captain at random. What is the probability the captain will be a forward?

    4. _____

5. What is the probability the captain will have an even-numbered jersey and will not be a forward?

    5. _____

6. On October 4, 2006, the Dow Jones Industrial Average rose 123.26 points to 11,850.61. What was the average at the start of the day?

    6. _____

7. **Multiple Choice** Which equation is represented by the graph below?

    7. _____

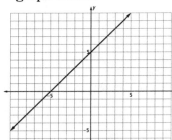

    A $y = -x + 5$ B $y = -x + -5$

    C $y - x = 5$ D $y - x = -5$

Chapter 5 Test Form B

8. Consider this problem: Samantha bought a computer for
$1,235. She added speakers that cost s dollars and a wireless
keyboard that cost $72, bringing the total cost to $1,455.
How much did the speakers cost?

   a. Write an equation to represent this problem.

   b. Solve your equation.

8. a. _____

   b. _____

9. **Multiple Choice** Which of the following is a solution of
   $x + -1.4 < \frac{26}{65}$?

   A $\frac{23}{65}$

   C 14

   B 2.8

   D 28

9. _____

10. The Ferris wheel pictured below is rotating
counterclockwise. Pedro is in the car marked P. The spoke
from the center of the wheel to Pedro's car forms an angle
of 65° with a vertical line. How many degrees does the
Ferris wheel need to rotate before Pedro is back to the
passenger-loading area?

10. _____

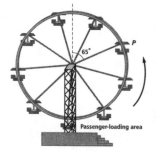

11. a. What addition is represented on the number line below?

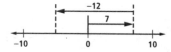

   b. What is the sum?

11. a. _____

    b. _____

12. Construct a triangle with the following side lengths:

   _____ c
   _____ d
   _____ e

12. _____

Chapter 5 Test **Form B**

13. Simplify the expression $f - g + (-g) - (-f)$.

13. _____

14. **Multiple Choice** Which property justifies the following
statement: If $p + 7 + n = 10$, then $7 + p + n = 10$?

14. _____

   A Commutative Property of Addition

   B Associative Property of Addition

   C Addition Property of Equality

   D Addition Property of Zero

In 15–17, consider the equation $6.46 - x = 10.32$.

15. Draw the fact triangle that represents this equation.

15.

16. Use the fact triangle to write two facts related to the original
equation.

16. _____

_____

17. Solve the equation for x.

17. _____

18. On Tuesday, a stock fell $2\frac{1}{4}$ points from its value on Monday.
On Wednesday, it rose $1\frac{1}{2}$ points. On Thursday, it rose
3 points. On Friday, it fell $2\frac{1}{2}$ points. What was the change in
the stock's value from Monday to Friday?

18. _____

19. Can a triangle have side lengths 38 inches, 73 inches, and
29 inches? Justify your answer.

19. _____

20. The library is 1.8 miles from the school and 3.2 miles from
the police station.

   a. Write a double inequality to represent the possible
   distances d between the school and the police station.

20. a. _____

   b. Graph the inequality on the number line.

   b.

Chapter 5 Test Form C

1. A triangle is to have sides of length 7 centimeters and 11 centimeters. Write an inequality to show the possible lengths of the third side. Then, choose one of the possible lengths and use a compass and straightedge to construct the triangle on a separate sheet of paper.

2. Draw a picture to help you explain why the results of these two additions are different.

   $-5 + 7 \qquad 5 + -7$

3. Choose three fractions from the box below whose sum is

   a. positive. b. negative. c. zero.

   Find each sum.

$\frac{3}{4}$	$-\frac{5}{12}$	$\frac{1}{4}$	$\frac{1}{3}$	$-\frac{1}{3}$	$\frac{1}{12}$

4. Write a word problem you can solve with the following equation. Then show how to use the equation to solve your problem.

   $p - 5 = -2$

5. Let x represent the probability that an event will occur. Let y represent the probability that it will not occur. Write an equation relating x and y. Graph your equation on grid paper, showing only the values that make sense in this situation.

6. a. Describe all the rotations whose measures m satisfy the equation $|m| = 90°$.

   b. Describe three pairs of rotations whose measures r and s satisfy the equation $|r + s| = 90°$. Consider both clockwise and counterclockwise rotations.

Name _____

You are helping a friend build a new personal-use robot. So far, the robot responds to the commands shown in the chart at the right. Each inch on paper represents a yard of actual movement. For instance, suppose the robot starts at its "home base" at the corner of the kitchen shown below. The arrow indicates the direction the robot faces at the start. This set of commands takes the robot along the dashed-line path to the refrigerator.

TURN followed by a number of degrees	
If the number is	*the turn is*
positive	counter-clockwise
negative	clockwise
zero	no turn

MOVE followed by a number of yards	
If the number is	*the move is*
positive	forward
negative	backward
zero	no move

TURN 45   MOVE $2\frac{1}{16}$ TURN –90   MOVE $4\frac{5}{8}$ TURN 45

a. Write a set of commands that will move the robot from its home base to face the sink. Then write a set of commands that will return the robot to its original position at home base.

b. What is the total distance that the robot travels in its round trip between home base and the sink?

c. Find three places in the kitchen to which the robot can move. For each location, write a set of commands that will move the robot there from its position at home base, and then return it to its original position. Calculate the distance the robot moves in that round trip. Organize your work so that your friend can read it easily and use it to program the robot.

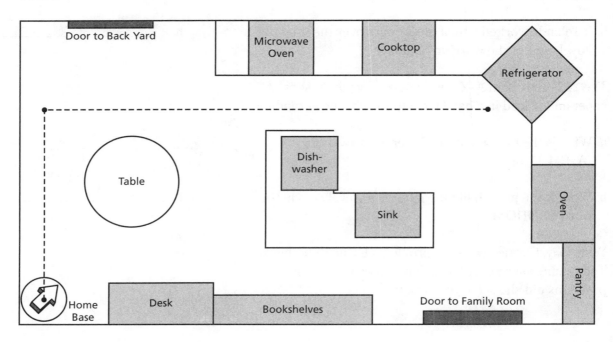

Chapter 5 Test Cumulative Form

In 1–3, simplify.

1. $-7.25 + (-3.5) - (-10.75) + 3.5$

1. _____

2. $|-9| + |5| + |9 + (-5)|$

2. _____

3. $4x - (-x + 7y)$

3. _____

In 4 and 5, solve.

4. $7 - (x + 3) = 14$

4. _____

5. $7\frac{1}{4} + x < 3\frac{1}{8}$

5. _____

6. Tuesday the high temperature was $67°$F. That was $13°$ greater than the high temperature m on Monday.

   a. Write an equation to represent this situation.

   6. **a.** _____

   b. Solve your equation to find Monday's high temperature.

   b. _____

7. Yolanda worked 3 hours on Friday, s hours on Saturday, and 8 hours on Sunday.

   a. Write an expression for the total number of hours Yolanda worked from Friday through Sunday.

   7. **a.** _____

   b. If Yolanda worked a total of 17 hours over the three days, how long did she work on Satuday?

   b. _____

8. The 26 letters from A–Z are written on separate slips of paper and placed in a hat. One letter is chosen at random.

   a. What is the probability the letter is a vowel (A, E, I, O, or U)?

   8. **a.** _____

   b. What is the probability the letter is a vowel *or* is in the word RANDOM?

   b. _____

9. Yesterday, Carmen solved P problems for math homework. Today, she solved only 5 problems. How many more problems did she solve yesterday?

   9. _____

Chapter 5 Test Cumulative Form

10. **Multiple Choice** Which of the following could be the side
lengths of a triangle?

10.

    A 7 inches, 3 inches, 5 inches   B 4 feet, 1 foot, 3 feet

    C 11 yards, 22 yards, 9 yards   D 8 miles, 8 miles, 18 miles

11. Consider this fact triangle.

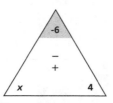

   a. Write three equations related to the fact triangle.

11. a.

_____

_____

   b. Find the value of x.

   b. _____

12. Graph the line with equation $x - y = -6$

12.

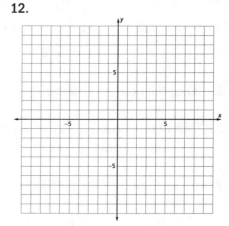

13. What single turn is equivalent to a 155° clockwise turn
followed by a 89° counterclockwise turn?

13. _____

14. What property justifies the following statement: Because
$\frac{1}{4} = 0.25$, it is also true that $x + \frac{1}{4} = x + 0.25$?

14. _____

15. Write 0.000000785 in scientific notation.

15. _____

Chapter 5 Test Cumulative Form

16. Give the ordered pair for a point in Quadrant II of the coordinate grid.

16. _____

17. What number does point A on the number line below represent?

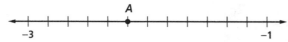

17. _____

18. Write $>$, $<$, or $=$ to make a true statement.

10.5 billion ____?____ 1.05×10^9

18. _____

19. Evaluate $\dfrac{x^3 + xy}{(3x - y)^2}$ when $x = 2$ and $y = 3$.

19. _____

20. An Olympic pool is 50 meters long and 25 meters wide. What is the diagonal distance across the pool to the nearest whole meter?

20. _____

21. Four instances of a pattern are given. Describe the general pattern using two variables.

21. _____

$$(3 + 5)^2 = 3^2 + 5^2 + 2 \cdot 3 \cdot 5$$
$$\left(\tfrac{1}{2} + \tfrac{1}{9}\right)^2 = \left(\tfrac{1}{2}\right)^2 + \left(\tfrac{1}{9}\right)^2 + 2 \cdot \tfrac{1}{2} \cdot \tfrac{1}{9}$$
$$(-1 + 7)^2 = (-1)^2 + 7^2 + 2 \cdot (-1) \cdot 7$$
$$(2.5 + 4.9)^2 = (2.5)^2 + 4.9^2 + 2 \cdot 2.5 \cdot 4.6$$

22. Graph all the solutions of $2 > x \geq -3$ on the number line.

22.

23. Mr. Park paid a $32 dinner bill and left an 18% tip. How much money did he pay in all?

23. _____

24. What digit is in the 15th decimal place of $0.\overline{5642}$?

24. _____

25. A square has an area of 51 square inches. What is the exact length of a side of the square?

25. _____

26. Simplify: $3\tfrac{3}{8} - 1\tfrac{5}{8} + 1\tfrac{3}{4}$.

26. _____

Chapter 5 Test **Cumulative Form**

27. Consider this statement:

    If a quadrilateral is a rectangle, then it is a trapezoid.

    a. Is the statement true? If not, give a counterexample. 27. **a.** _____

    b. Write the converse of the statement.

    _____

    c. Is the converse true? If not, give a counterexample. **c.** _____

28. **a.** Draw a pentagon and label the vertices. 28. **a.**

    b. Give three correct names for your pentagon. **b.** _____

29. Draw a Venn diagram to show the relationships among the 29.
    set of positive integers, the set of rational numbers, and the
    set of even numbers.

30. Let A be the set of all sports equipment and let B be the set
    of all hats.

    a. Name an item in $A \cap B$. 30. **a.** _____

    b. Name an item that is in A, but not in B. **b.** _____

    c. Name an item that is in B, but not in A. **c.** _____

Quiz Lessons 6-1 through 6-4

You will need a ruler and a protractor for this quiz.

1. Draw the translation image of the figure at the right under a translation 4 units right, and $3\frac{1}{2}$ units down.

1.

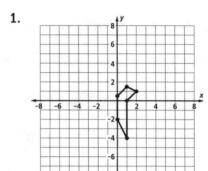

2. Rotate parallelogram *COWS* 60° about *H*.

2.

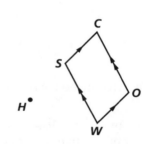

3. Draw all the lines of symmetry for the figure at the right.

3.

4. Reflect △*HEN* over $\overleftrightarrow{FX}$.

4.

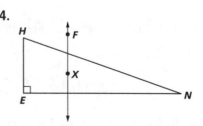

Name _____

5. Make a sketch to show how the figure at the right tessellates.

5.

6. Draw the reflection image of pentagon *ABCDE* over the *x*-axis. Then, reflect the image over the dashed line $x = -2$.

6.

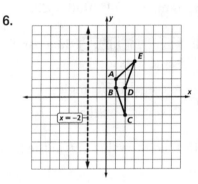

7. Determine the *n*-fold rotation symmetry of the figure.

a.

7. a. _____

b.

b. _____

Quiz Lessons 6-5 through 6-8

In 1–3, use the figure below. Lines *h* and *j* are parallel.

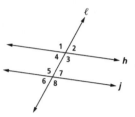

1. **Fill in the Blank** ∠1 and ∠4 are ____?____.

    1. _____

2. List all the angles with measure equal to m∠2.

    2. _____

3. If m∠6 = 74°, find m∠3.

    3. _____

4. **Multiple Choice** In a parallelogram, which angles have the same measure?

    4. _____

    A consecutive angles   B supplementary angles

    C vertical angles   D opposite angles

5. Find the value of *h* in the figure below.

    5. _____

6. **True or False** In a right triangle, the largest angle has a measure greater than 90°.

    6. _____

7. **Multiple Choice** If *WPRI* is the name of a parallelogram, which of the following must be true?

    7. _____

    A $WI = RI$

    B $\overline{PR} \parallel \overline{IW}$

    C $m\angle R = m\angle P$

    D ∠*W* and ∠*R* are supplementary.

8. The flap of a letter-sized envelope is a triangle with two 28° angles, as shown below. What is the measure of the other angle?

    8. _____

Chapter 6 Test Form A

You will need a ruler and a protractor for this test.

1. Reflect △*SET* over line *i*.

1.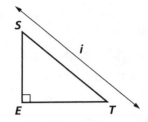

2. **True or False** The figure below tessellates.

2. _____

3. Name two pairs of congruent angles in the parallelogram below.

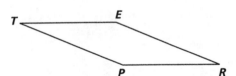

3. _____

In 4 and 5, use the figure below. Line *j* is parallel to line *ℓ*, line *m* is parallel to line *n*, and m∠4 = 38°.

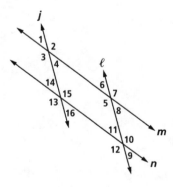

4. Find m∠11 + m∠9 + m∠3.

4. _____

5. Name a pair of alternate interior angles.

5. _____

6. **Multiple Choice** Which statement is true of triangles with two acute angles?

6. _____

   A The third angle is *always* obtuse.

   B The third angle is *sometimes, but not always* obtuse.

   C The third angle is *never* obtuse.

In 7–9, use the figure at the right.

7. Draw the image of this figure under the translation that maps (x, y) onto $(x + 2, y + -6)$. Label the image $A'M'F'O'C'E'U'S'I'$.

7, 8.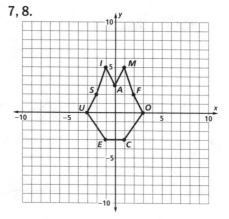

8. Reflect the original figure over the x-axis. Label the image $A^*M^*F^*O^*C^*E^*U^*S^*I^*$.

9. What is the distance between points E and M?

9. _____

10. Rotate $\triangle HEY -65°$ about T.

10.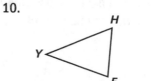

11. What is the value of c in the right triangle below?

11. _____

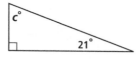

12. How many lines of symmetry does the oval below have?

12. _____

13. During a soccer game, Joseph (located at point *J*) passed the ball to William (at point *W*). William turned 64° to his left then passed the ball to Amber (at point *A*). Amber turned 13° to her left and passed the ball back to Joseph. (Assume a player is facing the kicker when he or she receives the ball.)

   a. Draw a diagram showing the path of the ball.   13. a.

   b. What is m∠*AJW*?   b. _____

In 14 and 15, use the parallelogram below.

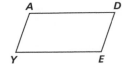

14. If *AY* = 17 cm and *DA* = 38 cm, what is the perimeter of the parallelogram?   14. _____

15. If m∠*A* = 108°, what is m∠*E*?   15. _____

16. **Multiple Choice** Which of the following shows the reflection image of *CAWL* over line *p*?   16. _____

A.   B.

C.   D.

17. What *n*-fold rotation symmetry does this figure have?   17. _____

18. Does the figure below tessellate? If so, draw the tessellation.   18. _____

In 19 and 20, use the figure below.

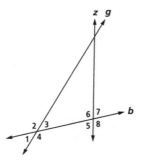

19. **True or False**   If m∠2 = 134° and m∠7 = 76°, then   19. _____
m∠2 + m∠3 > m∠7 + m∠6.

20. Is it possible for m∠3 + m∠6 to equal 180°? Explain why   20. _____
or why not.

Chapter 6 Test Form B

You will need a ruler and a protractor for this test.

1. Reflect △*NEW* over line *k*.

1.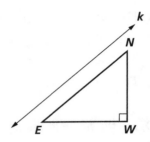

2. **True or False** The figure below tessellates.

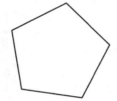

2. _____

3. Name two pairs of supplementary angles in the parallelogram below.

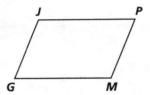

3. _____

In 4 and 5, use the figure below. Line *v* is parallel to line *w*, line *m* is parallel to line *n*, and m∠4 = 47°.

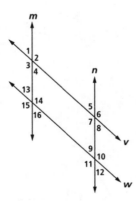

4. Find m∠6 + m∠7 + m∠13.

4. _____

5. Name a pair of corresponding angles.

5. _____

6. **Multiple Choice** Which statement is true of triangles with an obtuse angle?

6. _____

A The other two angles are *always* both acute.

B The other two angles are *sometimes, but not always* both acute.

C The other two angles are *never* both acute.

In 7–9, use the figure at the right.

7. Draw the image of this figure under the translation that maps (x, y) onto $(x + -3, y + 2)$. Label the image $J'K'L'M'N'P'Q'$.

7, 8.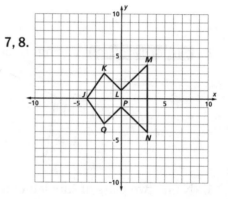

8. Reflect the original figure over the *y*-axis. Label the image $J*K*L*M*N*P*Q*$.

9. What is the distance between points Q and M?

9. _____

10. Rotate $\triangle PAL$ $-50°$ about C.

10.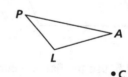

11. What is the value of v in the right triangle below?

11. _____

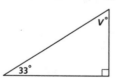

12. How many lines of symmetry does the parallelogram at right have?

12. _____

Chapter 6 Test Form B

13. Jen (located at point *J*) threw a ball to Wes (at point *W*). Wes turned 72° to his left then threw the ball to Aisha (at point *A*). Aisha turned 24° to her left and threw the ball back to Jen.

    a. Draw a diagram showing the path of the ball.

    13. a.

    b. What is m∠*AJW*?

    b. _____

In 14 and 15, use the parallelogram below.

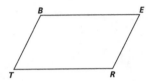

14. If *BT* = 15 cm and *TR* = 24 cm, what is the perimeter of the parallelogram?

    14. _____

15. If m∠*T* = 64°, what is m∠*B*?

    15. _____

16. **Multiple Choice** Which of the following shows the reflection image of *DART* over line *m*?

    16. _____

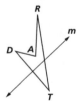

A. 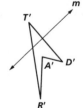   B.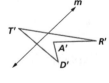

C. 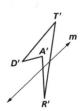   D.

Chapter 6 Test **Form B**

17. What *n*-fold rotation symmetry does this figure have?

17. _____

18. Does the figure below tessellate? If so, draw the tessellation.

18. _____

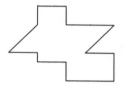

In 19 and 20, use the figure below.

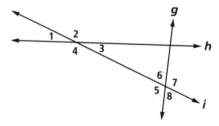

19. Is it possible for m∠3 + m∠6 to equal 180°? Explain why or why not.

19. _____

20. **True or False** If m∠1 = 25° and m∠5 = 110°, then m∠1 + m∠4 < m∠5 + m∠8.

20. _____

Chapter 6 Test   Form C

1. Complete the figure below so that line *m* is a line of symmetry. Then identify *all* lines of symmetry of your completed figure.

2. On a separate sheet of paper, write ten facts about the relationships among the lines and angles in the figure below.

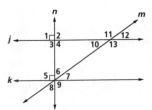

3. Suppose your friend draws parallelogram *CPTQ* but does not show it to you. He tells you that m∠C = 65°, *TQ* = 3 cm, and another side has length 5 cm. Do you have enough information to reproduce his parallelogram? If so, draw it and label all the side lengths and angle measures. If not, explain what additional information you need.

4. a. Reflect the figure at the right over line *p*. Does the union of the figure and its image have reflection symmetry? Explain.

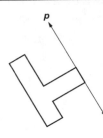

   b. Rotate the figure at the right 90° about point *P*. Does the union of the figure and its image have rotation symmetry? Explain.

Chapter 6 Test Form D

Your parents are planning to pave a rectangular patio floor with bricks. The floor is 5 feet wide and 7 feet long. The top surface of each brick is a rectangle that is 4 inches wide and 8 inches long.

Your parents have asked for your help in planning an attractive pattern for the floor. The figures on this page show seven patterns that are commonly used by bricklayers.

a. Which figures have reflection symmetry? Draw all the lines of symmetry in these figures.

b. Which figures have rotation symmetry? Determine the *n*-fold rotation symmetry of each of these figures.

c. Which figure is formed by translation images of the basic L-shape shown at the right?

d. According to the definition of tessellation you learned, which pattern is *not* a tessellation? Explain.

e. Choose one of the patterns on this page, or create your own original pattern. On graph paper, make a drawing that shows how the patio will look when it is completely covered with bricks arranged in your pattern. (You may need to use parts of bricks in some places.)

f. How many bricks are needed to cover the patio floor using the pattern you chose?

g. Bricks cost $1.28 each at your local building supply store. When you buy the bricks, you should get between 5% and 10% more than the plan shows to allow for breakage. Using this information, estimate the total cost of the bricks needed for the patio floor.

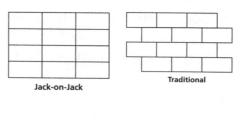

Jack-on-Jack   Traditional

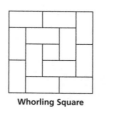
Whorling Square

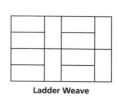
Ladder Weave

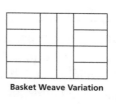
Basket Weave Variation

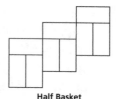
Half Basket

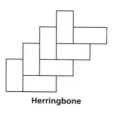
Herringbone

Chapter 6 Test Cumulative Form

You will need a ruler and a protractor for this test.

1. Reflect △*SAM* over line *k*.

1.

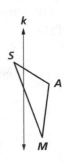

2. Rotate square *BTFQ* 120° about point *Q*.

2.

3. **Multiple Choice** Which figure does _not_ tessellate?

3. _____

A.

B.

C.

D.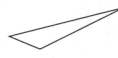

4. a. Draw all the lines of symmetry for the regular octagon at the right.

4. a.

b. Determine the _n_-fold rotation symmetry of the octagon.

b. _____

5. What is the greatest number of obtuse angles a triangle can have? Explain your answer.

5. _____

Chapter 6 Test Cumulative Form

6. In a parallelogram $ABCD$, $AB = 4$ feet, $AD = 6$ feet, and $m\angle B = 72°$. Give the lengths of the other two sides and the measures of the other three angles.

6. $BC =$ _____ $CD =$ _____

$m\angle A =$ _____ $m\angle C =$ _____

$m\angle D =$ _____

In 7 and 8, refer to the figure below.

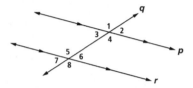

7. Name a pair of alternate exterior angles.

7. _____

8. Suppose $m\angle 6 = 49°$.

   a. Find $m\angle 1$.

   8. a. _____

   b. Find $m\angle 7$.

   b. _____

   c. Find $m\angle 3 + m\angle 2$.

   c. _____

9. Draw the image of $\triangle RED$ under the translation that maps (x, y) onto $(x + 4, y - 3)$.

9.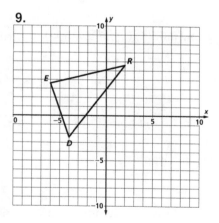

10. Refer to $\triangle RED$ in Question 9. What is the exact distance from point E to point R?

10. _____

11. Multiply and give the answer in scientific notation.

$$54.09 \times \frac{1}{100,000,000}$$

11. _____

12. Evaluate $7 + 21 \div \sqrt{7 \cdot 5 + 14}$.

12. _____

Chapter 6 Test   Cumulative Form

13. Three instances of a pattern are given. Describe the general pattern using two variables.

$$(5 - 2)(5 + 2) = 5^2 - 2^2$$

$$(0.3 - 5.9)(0.3 + 5.9) = 0.3^2 - 5.9^2$$

$$\left(\frac{3}{4} - \frac{1}{3}\right)\left(\frac{3}{4} + \frac{1}{3}\right) = \left(\frac{3}{4}\right)^2 - \left(\frac{1}{3}\right)^2$$

13. _____

14. Zoe's computer screen is 14 inches long and 9 inches wide. What is the length of the screen's diagonal to the nearest tenth of an inch?

14. _____

15. What number is represented by point P? Give your answer as a fraction and as a decimal.

15. _____

16. 125% of 36 = ____?____.

16. _____

17. Consider this statement:

   If a number is an integer, then it is a rational number.

   a. Is the statement true? If not, give a counterexample.

17. a. _____

   b. Write the converse of the statement.

   b. _____

   c. Is the converse true? If not, give a counterexample.

   c. _____

18. a. Graph the set of all numbers x such that $x \geq -1$ and $x \leq 3$.

18. a.

   b. Describe the solution set from Part a geometrically.

   b. _____

19. Last week, Ben earned M dollars mowing lawns. After spending $13 on a CD, he had $22 left.

   a. Write an equation to represent this situation.

19. a. _____

   b. Solve your equation to find out how much Ben earned last week.

   b. _____

20. Find the value of $|a + 6| - (-4) - b$ when $a = -10$ and $b = 16$.

20. _____

Comprehensive Test Chapters 1–6   page 1

1. $\dfrac{\sqrt{12 + 8 \div 2}}{3 \times 4} = $ _____?_____   1. _____

   A $\dfrac{\sqrt{10}}{12}$ B $\dfrac{1}{3}$

   C $\sqrt{\dfrac{5}{6}}$ D $\dfrac{5}{6}$

2. In scientific notation, $0.0047 \times 10^{13} = $ ___?___ .   2. _____

   A 4.7×10^{16} B 47×10^{9}

   C 4.7×10^{10} D $47{,}000{,}000{,}000$

3. In which quadrant of the coordinate grid is the point   3. _____
   $(4, -11)$?

   A I   B II

   C III   D IV

4. Which is the decimal form of 63.8 billion?   4. _____

   A 0.000000638 B $63{,}800{,}000$

   C $63{,}800{,}000{,}000$ D $63{,}800{,}000{,}000{,}000$

5. How is the number 3 being used in the following sentence?   5. _____
   Jack finished his homework 3 times as fast as Maya
   finished hers.

   A as a rate   B as a ratio

   C as a measure   D as an identification

6. Which of the following is a rational number?   6. _____

   A 3π B $\dfrac{5\pi}{2\pi}$

   C $\sqrt{3}$ D $\dfrac{3}{0}$

7. If $n = 4$ and $m = 6$, then $\dfrac{2^n + 3m}{(m - n)^2} = $ ___?___ .   7. _____

   A $\dfrac{17}{100}$ B $\dfrac{21}{2}$

   C $\dfrac{13}{2}$ D $\dfrac{17}{2}$

8. Nine less the square of a number can be written as ___?___ .   8. _____

   A $9 - n^2$ B $9 < n^2$

   C $n^2 - 9$ D $2n - 9$

9. If $a^{-2} = \dfrac{1}{a^2}$, then $5^{-2} = $ ___?___ .   9. _____

   A -25 B 25 C $-\dfrac{1}{25}$ D $\dfrac{1}{25}$

10. A queen-size mattress is 60 inches wide and 80 inches long.   10. _____
    Which is the length of the diagonal of a queen-size mattress?

    A 100 inches   B 140 inches

    C 280 inches   D 10,000 inches

Comprehensive Test Chapters 1–6

11. Which digit is in the 17th decimal place of $2.\overline{357}$?

11. _____

    A 2   **B** 3

    C 5   **D** 7

12. 225% of 40 is ____?____.

12. _____

    A 0.9   **B** 9

    C 90   **D** 900

13. Which inequality is graphed on the number line below?

13. _____

    A $-3 < x < 1$ **B** $-3 \le x \le 1$

    C $-3 < x \le 1$ **D** $-3 \le x < 1$

14. Which expression should be the entry in the empty cell of the table below?

14. _____

Column 1	Column 2
1	5
2	7
3	9
4	11
10	23
n	

    A $n + 2$

    B $4n + 1$

    C $2n + 3$

    D $5n$

15. $\sqrt{5} \cdot \sqrt{5} =$ ____?____

15. _____

    A 5   **B** 25

    C $2\sqrt{5}$ **D** $\sqrt{10}$

16. Raj has a $22\frac{1}{2}$-foot piece of speaker wire. He uses a $5\frac{3}{4}$-foot piece. How much speaker wire does he have left?

16. _____

    A $16\frac{3}{4}$ ft   **B** $17\frac{1}{4}$ ft

    C $17\frac{3}{4}$ ft   **D** $28\frac{1}{4}$ ft

17. Order the following numbers from least to greatest.

17. _____

    67%   6.7 $0.\overline{67}$ $\frac{2}{3}$

    A $\frac{2}{3}$, $0.\overline{67}$, 6.7, 67%   **B** $\frac{2}{3}$, 67%, $0.\overline{67}$, 6.7

    C $0.\overline{67}$, $\frac{2}{3}$, 67%, 6.7   **D** 6.7, $0.\overline{67}$, 67%, $\frac{2}{3}$

18. A bag contains only red, blue, and green marbles. The probability of selecting a red marble at random is $\frac{1}{3}$. The probability of selecting a blue marble is $\frac{5}{12}$. What is the probability of selecting a green marble?

    A $\frac{2}{3}$ B $\frac{1}{3}$

    C $\frac{1}{4}$ D Cannot be determined

18. _____

19. Geometrically, what is the set of all numbers x such that $x \leq -2$ or $x \geq -2$?

    A a point   B a segment

    C a ray   D a line

19. _____

20. Which figure is not a polygon?

    A.   B.

    C.   D.

20. _____

21. Which statement is false?

    A A rhombus is always a square.

    B A parallelogram is sometimes a rectangle.

    C A square is always a parallelogram.

    D A circle is never a polygon.

21. _____

22. To which of the following sets does the number 51 *not* belong?

    A odd numbers   B prime numbers

    C whole numbers   D integers

22. _____

23. Which term could go in the blank in the hierarchy below?

23. _____

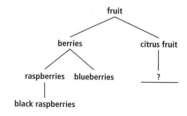

    A vegetables   B red raspberries

    C lemons   D melons

24. Which equation is an instance of the Property of Opposites?   24. _____

    A $-(-3.4) = 3.4$ B $-7 + 0 = -7$
    C $-\frac{1}{3} + \frac{1}{3} = 0$ D $8 + -2 = 8 - 2$

25. Simplify $-7 + 4 - |-7 + 4|$.   25. _____

    A -6 B 0
    C 6 D 8

26. A triangle has sides of length 11 inches and 5 inches. Which of the following could be the length of the third side?   26. _____

    A 4 inches   B 6 inches
    C 10 inches   D 16 inches

27. Luisa had t trading cards. After giving 8 cards to her brother, she had 31 cards left. Which equation represents this situation?   27. _____

    A $31 - 8 = t$ B $t + 8 = 31$
    C $31 - 8 = t$ D $t - 8 = 31$

28. Which equation does the graph below represent?   28. _____

    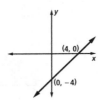

    A $x + y = 4$
    B $x + y = -4$
    C $x - y = -4$
    D $x - y = 4$

29. Which equation is *not* represented by the fact triangle below?   29. _____

    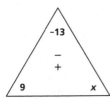

    A $9 - (-13) = x$
    B $9 + x = -13$
    C $-13 - 9 = x$
    D $-13 - x = 9$

30. Which single turn is equivalent to a 125° turn counterclockwise followed by a quarter turn clockwise?

    A 215° turn counterclockwise

    B 35° turn counterclockwise

    C 55° turn clockwise

    D 305° turn counterclockwise

    30. _____

31. How many lines of symmetry does a non-square rectangle have?

    A 1   B 2

    C 3   D 4

    31. _____

32. What is the distance between the points (−4, 1) and (2, 9)?

    A $\sqrt{74}$ B 10

    C $\sqrt{104}$ D $\sqrt{170}$

    32. _____

33. What is the value of x in the triangle below?

    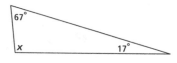

    A 48°   B 56.5°

    C 96°   D 103°

    33. _____

34. *ABCD* is a non-rectangular parallelogram. Which angles are *not* supplementary?

    A $\angle A$ and $\angle B$ B $\angle C$ and $\angle D$

    C $\angle A$ and $\angle D$ D $\angle A$ and $\angle C$

    34. _____

35. Point *T* has ordered pair (−2, 4). *T* is translated down 3 units and right 4 units. What is the ordered pair for its image?

    A (2, 1)   B (−5, 8)

    C (−6, 1)   D (2, 4)

    35. _____

36. Which figure tessellates?

    A regular pentagon   B regular octagon

    C scalene triangle   D circle

    36. _____

Quiz
Lessons 1-1 Through 1-4

1. $\frac{641}{1,000,000}$

2. a. 20.3
   b. people per square mile

3. C

4. a. 87
   b. years

5. identification

6. 4,096

7. $3^5 > 5^3$

8. E

9. a. positive
   b. negative

Quiz
Lessons 1-5 Through 1-8

1. a. division
   b. 31.74

2. 3.5×10^{-6}

3. D

4. 13.5

5. 243

6. 14

7. a. Sample answer:
   $($ 2 $+$ 5
   $)$ $\wedge$ 3 $\div$ $($ 16
   $-$ 2nd $\sqrt{}$ $($ 162 $\div$ 2
   $)$ $)$ ENTER

   b. 49

8. >

9. >

10. a. 0.0001
    b. 10^{-4}
    c. $\frac{1}{10,000}$

11. 11; left

Chapter 1 Test, Form A

1. $4^3 - 5 \cdot 2 = 64 - 5 \cdot 2 = 64 - 10 = 54$

2. $12^0 + \frac{8+3}{4 \cdot 22} = 12^0 + \frac{11}{4 \cdot 22} = 12^0 + \frac{11}{88} = 1 + \frac{11}{88} = 1\frac{1}{8}$ or 1.125

3. $\sqrt{9} - 2 \cdot (4 + 6) = 3 - 2 \cdot (4 + 6) = 3 - 2 \cdot 10 = 3 - 20 = -17$

4. $14{,}776.6 > 13{,}829.5 > 12{,}848.6$ or $12{,}848.6 < 13{,}829.5 < 14{,}776.6$

5.

6. 1.58164×10^{10}

7. No; 429.3 is not a value between 1 and 10.

8. 4,293,000

9. a. Answers vary. Sample:
   $($ 2nd $\sqrt{}$ 100
   $)$ $+$ 8 $)$ $/$ $($ 3
   $\wedge$ 2 $)$ ENTER

   b. 2

10. Answers vary. Sample: 1,950,000 users

11. Xmin: 1996; Xmax: 2005; Xscale: 1; Ymin: 0; Ymax: 2,500,000; Yscale: 500,000

12. B

13. a. (−5, 7)
    b. (3, 5)

c. (−1, −1)

d. (−4, −7)

e. (7, −3)

f. II

g. I

h. III

i. III

j. IV

14. a. 91.125
    b. 2,300,000,000,000
    c. 16.000017

15. a. five
    b. pairs of shoes

16. a. iii
    b. i

17. a. 0.00007081
    b. 7,081,000,000
    c. 0.007081
    d. 0.00007081

18. 1,087,101,569

19. a. zero
    b. positive integer
    c. negative integer

20. a. <
    b. =

Chapter 1 Test, Form B

1. $3^4 + 4 \cdot 2 = 81 + 4 \cdot 2 = 81 + 8 = 89$

2. $8^0 + \frac{11+7}{6 \cdot 12} = 8^0 + \frac{18}{6 \cdot 12} = 8^0 + \frac{18}{72} = 1 + \frac{18}{72} = 1\frac{1}{4}$ or 1.25

3. $\sqrt{25} - 3 \cdot (8 - 2) = 5 - 3 \cdot (8 - 2) = 5 - 3 \cdot 6 = 5 - 18 = -13$

4. $20{,}435.3 > 20{,}085.4 > 18{,}536.1$ or $18{,}536.1 < 20{,}085.4 < 20{,}435.3$

5.

6. 1.85326×10^{10}

7. No; 614.9 is not a value between 1 and 10.

8. 614,900

9. Sample answer:

(⎵4 + 2nd √
64))) ÷ 2 ^ 2
ENTER

b. 3

10. Answers vary. Sample: 1,800,000 users

11. Xmin: 1996; Xmax: 2005; Xscale: 1; Ymin: 0; Ymax: 2,500,000; Yscale: 500,000

12. D

13. a. $(-6, -2)$

b. $(4, -7)$

c. $(2, 6)$

d. $(-8, 3)$

e. $(-2, 2)$

f. III

g. IV

h. I

i. II

j. II

14. a. 1,785.0625

b. 7,320,000,000

c. 14.000020

15. a. three

b. cans of tennis balls

16. a. ii

b. i

17. a. 0.000006243

b. 624,300,000

c. 0.06243

d. 0.0000006243

18. 2,801,832,661

19. a. negative integer

b. zero

c. positive integer

20. a. $=$

b. $>$

Quiz
Lessons 2-1 through 2-3

1. $17 - x^2$

2. $180(a + b)$

3. p pounds of pasta makes $8p$ servings.

4.

Number of Loads	Cost
1	$1.50
2	$3.00
3	$4.50
4	$6.00
5	$7.50
n	$1.50n

5. $(7 + a) \cdot 5 = 7 \cdot 5 + a \cdot 5$

6. 5.009

7. ≈ 34.0816

8. Answers vary. Sample:
$4 + (5 + 9) = (4 + 5) + 9;$
$4 + (0 + 9) = (4 + 0) + 9;$
$4 + (11 + 9) = (4 + 11) + 9$

9. $D + 30$

Quiz,
Lessons 2-4 through 2-6

1. 41

2. C

3. $26.49

4. 68 inches

5. 3,200 units

6. a. $=(A6+C7+D4)/3$

b. 62

7. True; the tent is $\sqrt{8}$ m wide, which is less than 3 m.

Chapter 2 Test, Form A

1. D

2. D

3. 7

4. a. $43.93

b. $73.88

c. $601.00

5. $C = 5.99m + 2$

6. n cans of soup have $120n$ calories.

7. Answers vary. Sample:
$\frac{2}{3} + \frac{1}{2} = \frac{2 \cdot 2 + 1 \cdot 3}{3 \cdot 2};$
$\frac{1}{4} + \frac{1}{8} = \frac{1 \cdot 8 + 1 \cdot 4}{4 \cdot 8};$
$\frac{5}{9} + \frac{7}{13} = \frac{5 \cdot 13 + 7 \cdot 9}{9 \cdot 13}$

8. $(15 - n)^3$

9. $p \times 10^{-q} = p \times \frac{1}{10^q}$

10.

11.

12. a. C4–B4, 14.492;
=C5–B5, 6.781;
= C6–B6, 19.263

b. $=$SUM(D2:D6)$/5$ or
$=$(D2+D3+D4+D5
+D6)$/5$

13. $j = 10$

14. $-\frac{7}{3}$

15. 17,000 feet

16. B

17. No; $20^2 + 99^2 = 400$
$+ 9{,}801 = 10{,}201 \neq 10{,}000$
$= 100^2$

18. 73

19. $b = 640$

20. a.

Column 1	Column 2
1	3
2	5
3	7
4	9
8	17
10	21
900	1,801
n	$2n + 1$

b. The value in Column 2 is equal to the sum of 1 and the product of 2 and the value in Column 1.

Chapter 2 Test, Form B

1. B

2. B

3. 2

4. a. $19.03

   b. $30.48

   c. $232.00

5. $C = 2.29T + 3$

6. n spiral notebooks have $180n$ sheets.

7. Answers vary. Sample:
$\frac{2}{3} - \frac{1}{2} = \frac{2 \cdot 2 - 1 \cdot 3}{3 \cdot 2}$;
$\frac{1}{4} - \frac{1}{8} = \frac{1 \cdot 8 - 1 \cdot 4}{4 \cdot 8}$;
$\frac{5}{9} - \frac{7}{13} = \frac{5 \cdot 13 - 7 \cdot 9}{9 \cdot 13}$

8. $\frac{x - 12}{19}$

9. $\frac{p}{10^n} = p \times 10^{-n}$

10.
-1 0 3

11.
-3 0 1.5 3

12. a. $=$C4 + B4, $816.90; $=$C5 + B5, $440.65; C6 + B6, $1,130.25

   b. $=$SUM(D2:D6)$/5$ or $=$(D2 + D3 + D4 + D5 + D6)$/5$

13. $j = 20$

14. $-\frac{2}{3}$

15. 10,000 feet

16. C

17. No; $11^2 + 30^2 = 1021 \neq 32^2 = 1024$

18. 58

19. $w = 480$

20. a.

Column 1	Column 2
1	1
2	3
3	5
4	7
6	11
10	19
700	1,399
n	$2n - 1$

b. The value in Column 2 is equal to 1 less than 2 times the value in Column 1.

Chapter 2 Test, Cumulative Form

1. 17

2. 3

3. Answers vary. Sample: 2, 3

4. 9

5. $9 - 4n$

6. 34 ft

7. Yes; $20^2 + 21^2 = 841 = 29^2$

8. $\frac{3}{4}n = n - \frac{1}{4}n$

9. Answers vary. Sample:
$10 - (4 + 2) = 10 - 4 - 2$;
$40 - (17 + 13) = 40 - 17 - 13$

10. Going to the fair and riding n rides cost $5 + 2n$ dollars.

11. 75 yards

12.

Column 1	Column 2
1	3
2	8
3	13
4	18
5	23
9	43
n	$5n - 2$

13. 48 in.^{3}

14.
-5 -2 0 5

15.
-5 -4 0 5

16. 525.21875

17. 16,800,000,000

18. 4.32×10^{-5}

19. 7.383×10^6

20. 0.00109

21. 4,033

22. $16 + 7 \times 10 \div (4^2 - 11) =$
    $16 + 7 \times 10 \div (16 - 11) =$
    $16 + 7 \times 10 \div 5 = 16 + 70$
    $\div 5 = 16 + 14 = 30$

23. $5 > -5 > -12$

24. $\frac{407}{100}$

25. identification

26. rate

27. quadrant II

28. Sample answer:
    $(3, -5)$

29. about $1,800

30. 1995

Quiz
Lessons 3-1 through 3-3

1. 0.038, 0.0401, 0.333, 0.340

2. 5.00289, 5.00294, 5.003,
   5.00301

3. a. 9.599, 9.612, 9.706, 9.737

   b. Deferr

4. $\frac{984}{616} = \frac{123 \times 8}{77 \times 8}$, so the
   fractions are equal by the
   Equal Fractions Property.

5. Answers vary. Sample:
   1.39, 1.48006

6. $>$

7. $42\frac{5}{7}$

8. $1\frac{23}{30}$

9. $11\frac{7}{12}$

10. $3\frac{26}{45}$

11. $7\frac{1}{8}$ inches

Quiz
Lessons 3-4 through 3-6

1. Estimate; the number has
   most likely been rounded
   to the nearest ten.

2. $3.6\overline{717}$

3. 5 cm

4. 20% + 75%

5. D

6. false

7. Pat; $\frac{1}{3} = 0.\overline{3} > 33\% =$
   $0.33 > 0.3$

8. 8,000

9. $\frac{47}{60}$

10. 25%

Chapter 3 Test, Form A

1. C

2. 1.5

3. He rounded down.

4. a. $\frac{555}{673}$

   b. 82.5%

5. 1.5625

6. $16.41\overline{6}$

7. a. $\frac{14}{55}$

   b. $0.2\overline{54}$

   c. 5

8. a. $<$

   b. $<$

   c. $=$

9. a. 0.1 units

   b.
      6.8   7.15   7.88 8

10. $\frac{1}{6}$

11. 0.063

12. Answers vary. Sample:
    about $2.90

13. $\frac{1}{2}$

14. a. $0.32

    b. 3 gross

15. $28.67

16. 6.557

17. Yes; $5\frac{2}{3} = \frac{17}{3}$ and by
    the Equal Fractions
    Property, $\frac{17}{3} = \frac{17 \times 2}{3 \times 2} = \frac{34}{6}$.

18. $4.92\overline{34}$

19. 34% + 17%

20. a. 7 feet

    b. 9.9 feet

21. 24%

22. $1\frac{35}{132}$

Chapter 3 Test, Form B

1. B

2. He rounded down.

3. a. $\frac{118}{673}$

   b. about 17.5%

4. 1.5

5. 2.0625

6. $9.\overline{63}$

7. a. $\frac{13}{55}$

   b. $0.2\overline{36}$

   c. 3

8. a. $=$

   b. $>$

   c. $<$

9. a. 0.2 units

 b.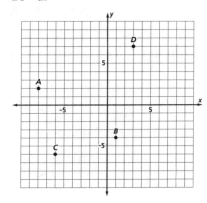
  (number line marked 5.6, 5.9, 6.45, 7)

10. $\frac{5}{6}$

11. 0.049

12. Answers vary. Sample: about $1.20

13. $\frac{2}{3}$

14. a. $0.59

 b. 9 packs

15. $31.59

16. 8.185

17. Yes; $2\frac{3}{8} = \frac{19}{8}$ and by the Equal Fractions Property, $\frac{19}{8} = \frac{19 \times 3}{8 \times 3} = \frac{57}{24}$.

18. $1.48\overline{382}$

19. 7% + 81%

20. a. 6 ft

 b. 8.5 ft

21. 18%

22. $1\frac{2}{21}$

Chapter 3 Test, Cumulative Form

1. $5\frac{1}{12}$

2. $\frac{16}{35}$

3. $1\frac{9}{56}$

4. $\frac{8}{9}$

5. −0.78, −0.078, −0.0078

6. $\frac{1}{3}, \frac{4}{11}, \frac{5}{13}$

7. $4.27, 4.\overline{27}, 4.2\overline{7}$

8. $-\frac{7}{12}, -\frac{5}{9}, -\frac{1}{2}$

9. a. $\sqrt{42}$ units

 b. 6.48 units

10. $2.79

11. a. $\frac{2}{3}$

 b. 0

12. a. 2.41

 b. 2.45

13. $\frac{3,409}{1,000}$

14. 0.9%

15. a. 32.8

 b. 32.5

16 a.

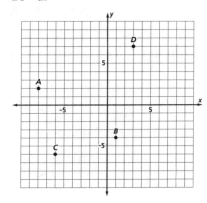

 b. Quadrant II

17. 6.364×10^{-7}

18. 4.55659×10^7

19. $(14 - 6)^2 + 27 \div 3 = 8^2 + 27 \div 3 = 64 + 27 \div 3 = 64 + 9 = 73$

20. rate; words and minutes

21. ratio

22. −7, −3, 0, 3

23. 29

24. $\frac{a+b}{c} = \frac{a}{c} + \frac{b}{c}$

25. (number line from −3 to 3, open circle at −1, closed at 3.5)

26. $\frac{1}{7}$

27. $7(m + 12)^2$

28. a. 11

 b. 14

c. 17

d. 302

e. $3n + 2$

29. $x = 12$

30. Answers vary. Sample: 12, 13

Chapters 1–3, Comprehensive Test

1. D
2. C
3. D
4. B
5. A
6. B
7. D
8. D
9. C
10. A
11. B
12. B
13. D
14. A
15. A
16. C
17. C
18. D
19. C
20. B
21. B
22. A
23. B
24. C

25. C

26. C

27. B

28. D

29. C

30. B

31. D

32. C

Quiz,
Lessons 4-1 through 4-3

1. False; Sample
   counterexample: 120

2. never

3. sometimes but not always

4. Answers vary.
   Sample: If a polygon
   is a square, then it is a
   rectangle.

5. I saw something.

6. D

7. −1.9

8. a. You hit your little
      brother.

   b. You will be in trouble.

   c. If you are in trouble,
      then you hit your little
      brother.

Quiz,
Lessons 4-4 through 4-6

1. a. {2}

   b. {0, 2, 3, 4, 5, 6, 7, 8}

2.

3.
   $\frac{5}{4}$

4. false

5. true

6. true

7. a. pentagon

   b. Sample answer: S

   c. Sample answer: $\overline{AR}$

   d. Answers may vary.
      Sample: *MARKS, RKSMA*

Chapter 4 Test, Form A

1. $m = 13$; Additive Identity
   Property

2. $n = -4$; Op-Op Property

3. sometimes but not always

4. sometimes but not always

5. always

6. always

7. a. the set of all monkeys

   b. the set of all animals

8. false

9. false

10. a. If the barbeque is ruined,
       then there will have been
       a thunderstorm.

    b. no

11. a. A polygon is a figure
       with sides and angles.

    b. No; Sample explanation:
       It does not specify that
       a polygon encloses a
       single region.

12. a.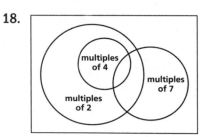

    b. line segment

13.

14. $q < 2.37$

15. a. quadrilateral

    b. $\overline{AB}, \overline{BC}, \overline{CD}, \overline{DA}$

    c. Sample answer: *ABCD,*
       CDAB

16. Sample answer: −8

17. A polygon encloses space
    in a single plane.

18.

19. Hypothesis: A polygon
    has exactly 12 sides.
    Conclusion: It is a
    dodecagon.

20.

21.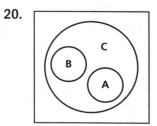

22.

```
                real numbers
              /              \
        rational          irrational
        numbers           numbers
           |
        integers
           |
         whole
        numbers
```

23. ∠*DEW*, ∠*WED*, ∠*E*

24. a. If an animal has four legs, then it is a dog.

b. Sample answer: A cat is an animal that has four legs, but it is not a dog.

Chapter 4 Test, Form B

1. $p = 0.67$; Additive Inverse Property

2. $v = 0$; Additive Identity Property

3. always

4. always

5. sometimes but not always

6. never

7. a. ∅

b. the set of all fish and all mammals

8. true

9. false

10. a. If you hear music, then you are at a rock concert.

b. no

11. a. A parallelogram is a quadrilateral with parallel sides.

---

b. No; Sample explanation: It does not specify that a parallelogram has two pairs of parallel sides.

12. a.

b. line segment

13.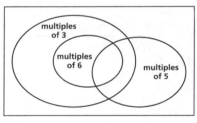

14. $x > 2.33$

15. a. pentagon

b. $\overline{ST}, \overline{TU}, \overline{UV}, \overline{VW}, \overline{WS}$

c. Sample answer: *STUVW*; *UVWST*

16. Answers may vary. Sample: 2.7

17. The segments don't intersect at their endpoints only.

18.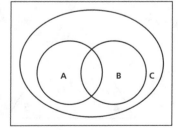

19. Hypothesis: A quadrilateral has four right angles. Conclusion: It is a rectangle.

20.

21.

22.

```
                real numbers
              /              \
        rational          irrational
        numbers           numbers
           |
        integers
           |
         whole
        numbers
```

23. ∠*YBC*, ∠*CBY*, ∠*B*

24. a. If a food is a vegetable, then it is green.

b. Sample answer: A carrot is a vegetable, but it is not green.

Chapter 4 Test, Cumulative Form

1. a. {1, 2, 3, 4, 6, 9, 12, 18, 27, 36}

b. {1, 3, 9}

2. Sample answer:

3. always

4. sometimes but not always

5. Additive Identity Property

6. Opposite of Opposites (or Op-Op) Property

7. a. An animal is a horse.

b. It has hooves.

c. If an animal has hooves, then it is a horse.

d. No; Sample counterexample: Goats have hooves.

8. Sample answer:

9. If a whole number is the greatest common factor of two numbers, then it is the greatest whole number that is a factor of both numbers.

If a number is the greatest whole number that is a factor of two numbers, then it is the greatest common factor of the two numbers.

10. Sample answer: -6π

11. Sample answer: 7

12.

13.

14.

15.

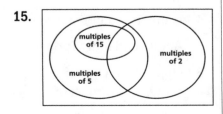

16. 4.7×10^{-6}

17. 18,700,000,000,000

18. quadrant II

19. 1

20. 8.337×10^{14}

21. Sample answer: 0, 4

22. $11n + 5$

23. true

24. 25 cm²

25. With tax, a d dollar item costs $d + 0.06 \times d$ dollars.

26. 3,702,000.002

27. $5\frac{23}{56}$

28. $0.8\overline{3}$; $83\frac{1}{3}\%$

29. $\overline{)54}$ cm

30. $\frac{6}{25}$

Quiz
Lessons 5-1 through 5-4

1. -8

2. -4

3. 6

4. 0

5. a.

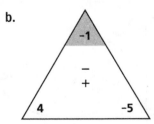

b.

6. Commutative Property of Addition

---

7. $b + c + d = v$

8. $22 million

9. $100 - T$

10. $a + -b$

Quiz
Lessons 5-5 through 5-8

1. $r = 3$

2. $x = \frac{1}{2}$

3. $t \le 92$

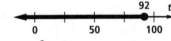

4. $p < \frac{6}{5}$

5. Addition Property of Equality

6.

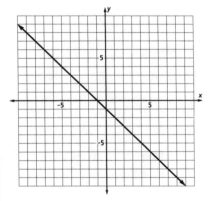

7. a. $\frac{1}{6}$

   b. $\frac{1}{4}$

   c. $\frac{1}{12}$

   d. $\frac{1}{3}$

8. a. $13.72 + d = 14.4$

   b. 0.68 sec

Chapter 5 Test, Form A

1. -7.25
2. 9
3. 13.2
4. $\frac{1}{3}$
5. $\frac{1}{6}$
6. $2{,}246.74$
7. D
8. a. $3{,}250 + t + 178 = 3{,}587$
   b. $\$159$
9. D
10. $215°$
11. a. $(-14) + (-8)$
    b. -22
12.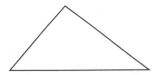
13. $2a$
14. C
15.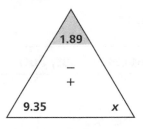
16. $1.89 - x = 9.35$;
    $1.89 - 9.35 = x$
17. $x = -7.46$
18. $+5$ inches
19. No; $8 + 10 = 18 < 19$
20. a. $1.2 \le d \le 4.4$
    b. [number line with points at 1.2 and 4.4]

Chapter 5 Test, Form B

1. -6
2. $34\frac{8}{13}$
3. 9.6
4. $\frac{3}{8}$
5. $\frac{1}{4}$
6. $11{,}727.35$
7. C
8. a. $1{,}235 + s + 72 = 1{,}455$
   b. $\$148$
9. A
10. $245°$
11. a. $7 + (-12)$
    b. -5
12. Note: 50% of actual size

13. $2f - 2g$
14. A
15.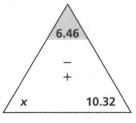
16. $x + 10.32 = 6.46$;
    $6.46 - 10.32 = x$
17. $x = -3.86$
18. $-\frac{1}{4}$ point
19. No; $29 + 38 = 67 < 73$
20. a. $1.4 \le d \le 5$
    b. [number line with points at 1.4 and 5]

Chapter 5 Test, Cumulative Form

1. 3.5
2. 18
3. $5x - 7y$
4. $x = -10$
5. $x < -4\frac{1}{8}$
6. a. Equation should be equivalent to $m + 13 = 67$.
   b. $54°$ F
7. a. $3 + s + 8$
   b. 6 hours
8. a. $\frac{5}{26}$
   b. $\frac{9}{26}$
9. $P - 5$ problems
10. A
11. a. $x + 4 = -6$; $-6 - x = 4$;
    $-6 - 4 = x$
    b. $x = -10$
12.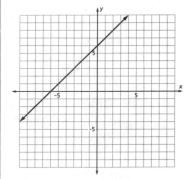
13. a $66°$ clockwise turn
14. Addition Property of Equality
15. 7.85×10^{-7}
16. Sample answer: $(-5, 2)$

17. $-2\frac{1}{6}$

18. $>$

19. $\frac{14}{9}$

20. 56 m

21. $(x + y)^2 = x^2 + y^2 + 2xy$

22.

23. $37.76

24. 4

25. $\sqrt{51}$ in.

26. $3\frac{1}{2}$

27. a. yes

b. If a quadrilateral is a trapezoid, then it is a rectangle.

c. no; Sample counterexample:

28. a. Sample answer:
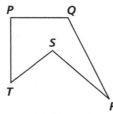

b. Sample names for pentagon above: *PQRST*, *RSTPQ*, *PTSRQ*

29.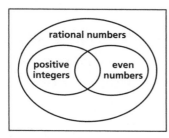

30. a. Sample answer: football helmet

b. Sample answer: tennis racquet

c. Sample answer: beret

Quiz,
Lessons 6-1 through 6-4

1.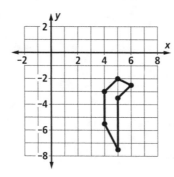

2.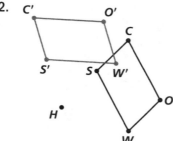

3.

4.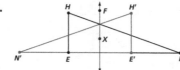

5.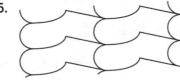

6.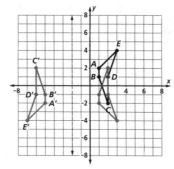

7. a. 3

b. 6

Quiz
Lessons 6-5 through 6-8

1. a linear pair, supplementary angles, or adjacent angles

2. $\angle4, \angle6, \angle7$

3. $106°$

4. D

5. $78°$

6. false

7. B

8. $124°$

Chapter 6 Test, Form A

1.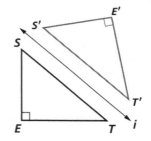

2. true

3. $\angle E$ and $\angle P$; $\angle T$ and $\angle R$

4. $218°$

5. Sample answer: $\angle5$ and $\angle10$

6. B

7.

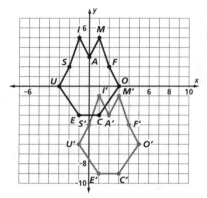

8.

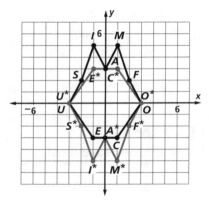

9. $\sqrt{68}$ units

10.

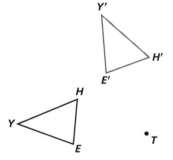

11. 69

12. 2

13. a.

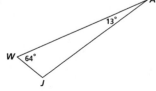

b. 103°

14. 110 cm

15. 108°

16. D

17. 7

18.

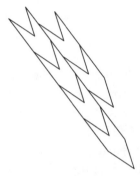

19. false

20. No; Sample explanation: ∠3 and ∠6 are two angles of a triangle. Because the sum of three angles in a triangle must be 180°, the sum of these two angles must be less than 180°.

Chapter 6 Test, Form B

1.

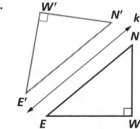

2. false

3. Sample answer: ∠G and ∠J; ∠J and ∠P

4. 313°

5. Sample answer: ∠14 and ∠2

6. A

7.

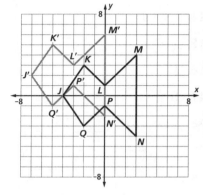

8.

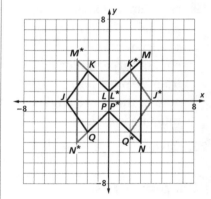

9. $\sqrt{74}$ units

10.

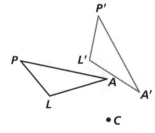

11. 57°

12. 0

13. a.

b. 84°

14. 78 cm

15. 116°

16. B

17. 8

18. yes;

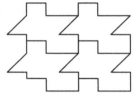

19. No; Sample explanation:
∠3 and ∠6 are two angles
of a triangle. Because the
sum of three angles in a
triangle must be 180°, the
sum of these two angles
must be less than 180°.

20. false

**Chapter 6 Test,
Cumulative Form**

1.

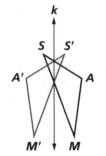

2.

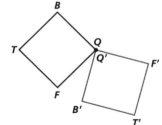

3. C

4. a.

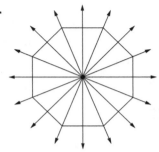

b. 8

5. 1; Sample explanation:
The measures of the three
angles of a triangle add
to 180°. If one angle has
a measure greater than
90°, then there is less than
90° left for the other two
angles. So, each of the
other two angles must be
less than 90°.

6. $BC = 6$ ft; $CD = 4$ ft; m∠A
$= 108°$; m∠$C = 108°$;
m∠D $= 72°$

7. Sample answer: ∠1 and ∠8

8. a. 131°

b. 49°

c. 98°

9.

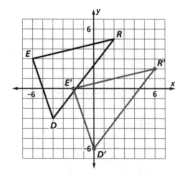

10. $\sqrt{68}$ units

11. 5.409×10^{-7}

12. 10

13. $(a - b)(a + b) = a^2 - b^2$

14. 16.6 inches

15. $-4\frac{5}{6}$; $-4.8\overline{3}$

16. 45

17 a. yes

b. If a number is a rational
number, then it is an
integer.

c. No; Sample
counterexample: 0.5 is a
rational number, but it is
not an integer.

18. a.

$$\begin{array}{ccccccccc} \text{-2} & \text{-1} & 0 & 1 & 2 & 3 & 4 & 5 & 6 \end{array} \quad x$$

b. line segment

19. a. $M - 13 = 22$

b. $35

20. −8

**Chapter 1–6
Comprehensive Test**

1. B

2. C

3. D

4. C

5. B

6. B

7. D

8. A

9. D

10. A

11. C

12. C

13. D

14. C

15. A

16. A
17. B
18. C
19. D
20. B
21. A
22. B
23. C
24. C
25. A
26. C
27. D
28. D
29. A
30. B
31. B
32. B
33. C
34. D
35. A
36. C

Chapter 1 Test Form C   Evaluation Guide

1. Explain how you know that 7.25 is a rational number. Then, write a sentence in which this number is used as a rate and a sentence in which it is used as a measure.

Objectives G, J
- Demonstrates an understanding of the meaning of rational number.
- Uses 7.25 as a rate; Sample answer: Tom rode his bike 7.25 miles per hour.
- Uses 7.25 as a measure; Sample answer: The room was 7.25 meters long.

2. Which of these numbers are equal? Which number is in scientific notation? Explain your answers.

89.7 millionths   0.000897
89.7×10^{-7} 8.97×10^{-5}

Objectives B, D, E, H
- Demonstrates a logical strategy for comparing numbers given in different forms.
- Understands scientific notation.
- Identifies 89.7 millionths and 8.97×10^{-5} as the equal numbers.
- Identifies 8.97×10^{-5} as the number in scientific notation.

3. See page 9.

Objectives C, J
- Knows the order of operations.
- Evaluates the expression to get 52.
- Uses the result as a count; Sample answer: There were 52 people at the class picnic.
- Uses the result as a code or location; Sample answer: Kaya lives at 52 Maple Lane.

4. See page 9.

Objectives F, I, L
- Interprets the situation in terms of positive and negative numbers.
- Forms the inequality $-3 < -2.25 < 6.5$.
- Locates values on a number line.

5. Evaluate 4.8^5 by using your calculator. Then, without actually multiplying, tell what power of 10 you would need to multiply the result by to move the digit 4 to the millions place. Explain how you found your answer.

Objectives A, B, D
- Demonstrates the ability to use the exponent key on a calculator.
- Demonstrates an understanding of how to multiply a decimal number by a power of 10.
- Demonstrates an understanding of place value.
- Evaluates 4.8^5 to get 2548.03968
- Identifies 10^5 as the power of 10 needed to move 4 to the millions place.

6. Explain how you can determine what quadrant a point is in simply by looking at its ordered pair. If you are told a point is not in any quadrant, what can you say about its ordered pair?

Objective M
- Understands how the signs of the x- and y-coordinates of a point relate to the quadrant the point is in.
- Knows that a point that is not in any quadrant must have at least one coordinate that is 0.
- Provides a clear, correct explanation.

Name _____

Chapter 1 Test Form D   Evaluation Guide

Teacher Notes

Objective K

Concepts and Skills This activity requires students to:

- interpret data given in a table.
- make a scatter plot of real data.
- describe trends in data shown on a scatter plot.
- compare two sets of data plotted on the same axes.

Guiding Questions

- What does the pattern in the points for males tell you about how the number of bachelor's degrees has changed over the years? What about the pattern in the points for females?
- How did the number of degrees awarded to males and females compare in 1977? How did this change over the years that followed?

Answers

a.

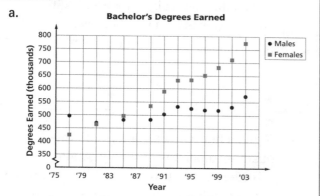

Bachelor's Degrees Earned

b. Answers vary. Sample: Males began at about 500,000 and stayed fairly steady withf a slight increase to 570,000 by 2003. Females started at 424,000 and increased continuously, reaching 775,000 by 2003. Females constantly increased over the years while males stayed fairly level and at times decreased. Females surpassed males in 1979 and continued constantly gaining. Prediction for 2013: Males 625,000; Females 862,000.

Evaluation

Level	Standard to be achieved for performance at specified level
5	Student neatly and accurately plots the data from the table. Student completely and correctly addresses the first three required points. Student makes a reasonable prediction about 2013 and supports it with information from the graph.
4	Student neatly and accurately plots the data from the table. Student addresses the first three required points, but may miss one or two key features of the plots. Student makes a reasonable prediction for 2013 and supports it with information from the graph.
3	Student plots one or two of the points inaccurately. Student attempts to address the first three required points, but misses one or two key features of the plot. Student makes a reasonable prediction for 2013 but does not support it.
2	Student makes several mistakes when plotting the points. Student attempts to address at least one of the required points, but misses several key features of the plot. Student makes an unreasonable prediction and does not support it.
1	Student's plot is messy and inaccurate. Student makes little or no attempt to address the required points.

Extensions

Have students choose a specific field of study (for example, science, engineering, or history) and research how the number of degrees in that field have changed over the years. Have students make a scatter plot of their data and write a paragraph describing any interesting trends.

A16   *Transition Mathematics*

Chapter 2 Test Form C   Evaluation Guide

1. Evaluate $p^2 - 3$ when $p = 2$, $p = 3$, and $p = 4$. Which of these values are solutions of $p^2 - 3 = 10$? Which are solutions of $p^2 - 3 < 10$? Which are solutions of $p^2 - 3 \geq 10$? Explain your answers.

Objectives A, B
- Correctly evaluates expression to get 1, 6, and 13.
- Understands what a solution of an equation or inequality is.
- Recognizes that none of the given numbers are solutions of $p^2 - 3 = 10$.
- Identifies 2 and 3 as solutions of $p^2 - 3 < 10$.
- Identifies 4 as a solution of $p^2 - 3 \geq 10$.

2. For each number line, write an inequality that describes the graph.
Graph the points that are on both number lines above and write a double inequality to describe the graph.

Objective J
- Demonstrates an understanding of graphs of inequalities.
- Writes $x < 2$ to describe the first graph.
- Writes $x \geq -1$ to describe the second graph.
- Correctly graphs the points that are on both number lines.
- Writes the double inequality $-1 \leq x < 2$ to describe the last graph.

3. See page 19.

Objectives D, I
- Understands that solving the problem involves using the Pythagorean Theorem.
- Applies the Pythagorean Theorem to find that the length of the diagonal is 150.
- Provides a clear, logical explanation for why Rafi's claim is impossible; Sample answer: The total length of one "lap" is 360 m. Because 360 does not divide evenly into 1600, Rafi cannot be correct.

4. See page 19.

Objectives G, L
- Demonstrates ability to recognize and extend a pattern in a table.
- Is able to calculate the value of a variable given the values of other variables in a formula.
- Concludes that Roscoe's is less expensive.
- Provides a correct and logical explanation for answer.

5. See page 19.

Objectives E, G
- Is able to give two more instances of the patterns.
- Is able to write a description of the pattern using variables. Sample answer: An n-foot by m-foot pond requires $2 \cdot n + 2 \cdot m + 4$ tiles.

Chapter 2 Test Form D   Evaluation Guide

Teacher Notes

Objectives A, B, F, J, H

Concepts and Skills This activity requires students to:

- read information from text and a table.
- make decisions based on given data and real-life experiences.
- calculate the value of a variable given the values of other variables in a formula.
- write descriptions of real-world patterns using variables.
- evaluate algebraic expressions.
- find solutions to equations.
- compare and perform operations with decimals.
- prepare a written and graphic summary of results.

Guiding Questions

- How can you work with the prices when some are given as dollars and others are given as cents?
- How does your answer to Part b help in writing an equation for Part c?

Answers

a. $2.60; $4.60; $11.30; $4.00; $1.00; $2.00; $0.30; $0.50; $0.30

b. $2.60 \cdot 2 = $5.20; $2.60 \cdot 3 = $7.80; $2.60 \cdot 4 = $10.40; $2.60n

c. $2.60n = 65$; $n = 25$; 25 T-shirts

d. Solving $2.60n = 50$ gives $1 \approx 19.23$, so 20 T-shirts is the least number that would yield at least $50 profit.

e. Answers vary.

Evaluation

Level	Standard to be achieved for performance at specified level
5	The student demonstrates a clear understanding of expressions and equations and a keen sense of the given situation. All calculations are accurate and complete. The written report and the graph are thorough, well-organized, and easy to read.
4	The student demonstrates a clear understanding of expressions and equations and a sound grasp of the given situation. The student performs all necessary calculations, but may make some minor errors. The written report and the graph are well-organized and easy to read, but reflect the minor computational errors.
3	The student demonstrates a fundamental understanding of expressions and equations, but may need some assistance in getting started. The student understands the nature of the calculations needed, but there may be one or more major errors or omissions. The written report and the graph reflect these errors, and they may be somewhat disorganized and difficult to read.
2	The student has some understanding of expressions and equations, but can apply them to the given situation only with a great deal of assistance. There are several major errors or omissions in the student's calculations. The student attempts to prepare a written report and a graph, but the results are jumbled and incomplete.
1	The student demonstrates little if any understanding of expressions and equations and, even when prompted, cannot apply them to the given situation. The student attempts some calculations, but they are superfluous or irrelevant. The student may prepare a written report simply by copying the given information, and there is no meaningful effort to draw a graph.

Extensions

Give students the formula $M = \frac{P}{W} \times 100$, where P is profit, W is wholesale price, and M is percent of markup. Have students estimate the standard percent of markup that was used for items of clothing (about 50%) and for supplies (about 75%). Have them suggest several additional imprint items that might be offered in the bookstore, estimate a wholesale price for each, and use the standard percents of markup to calculate appropriate retail prices.

Chapter 3 Test Form C   Evaluation Guide

1. See page 32.

_____ > _____ > _____

Objectives A, H
- Demonstrates an understanding of the raised bar symbol for repeating decimals.
- Gives an appropriate explanation.
- Fills in the blanks to create the statement $0.2\overline{4} > 0.\overline{24} > 0.24$.

2. See page 32.

Objectives B, G, J
- Demonstrates an understanding of the Equal Fractions Property.
- Understands how to add fractions.
- Makes an appropriate drawing, such as the one below.

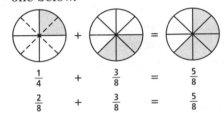

$$\frac{1}{4} + \frac{3}{8} = \frac{5}{8}$$

$$\frac{2}{8} + \frac{3}{8} = \frac{5}{8}$$

3. See page 32.

Objectives C, K
- Can round decimals up or down to the nearest value of a decimal place.
- Is able to deal with estimates in real situations.
- Gives appropriate examples. Sample example: If 3 pens cost $5, 1 will cost $1.67. If an elevator can safely carry 2,350 lb, 2,300 is a safer weight than 2,400 lb.

4. See page 32.

Objectives D, I
- Knows common fraction, decimal, and percent equivalents.
- Demonstrates and ability to multiply by 0.1, 0.01, 0.001, and so on.
- Gives an appropriate reason for each step:
  Step 1: Substitution Principle
  Step 2: Meaning of percent
  Step 3: Arithmetic

5. See page 32.

Objective E
- Knows how to find the percent of a number.
- Can compute the new total after a percent increase or decrease.
- Recognizes that the final price will *not* be equal to the original price, regardless of what the original price is.
- Provides a correct explanation of why the prices are not equal. Sample explanation: When you compute the decrease, you are finding 10% of a greater price, so the amount of the decrease is greater than the amount of the increase.

6. See page 32.

Objectives A, L, M, O
- Understands the geometric definition of square root.
- Can estimate square roots.
- Knows how to compute the probability of an event when outcomes are equally likely.
- Gives the probability as $\frac{3}{5}$.
- Writes an appropriate problem and gives the correct answer. Sample problem: What is the probability that the side length is less than 4? Answer: $\frac{1}{5}$.

Chapter 3 Test Form D   Evaluation Guide

Teacher Notes

Objectives A, D, E, G

Concepts and Skills This activity requires students to:

- read, interpret, and analyze data presented in a circle graph.
- make decisions concerning the appropriate presentation of data.
- convert among fractions, decimal, and percents.
- find percents of quantities.
- summarize results.

Guiding Questions

- Why is it important that all three graphs be labeled in the same way?
- How can you check that you have labeled the graphs correctly?

Answers

a., e. Answers may vary.

b. Grade 6 sectors: D) 10%, $\frac{1}{10}$; Ca) 35%, $\frac{7}{20}$; M) 20%, $\frac{1}{5}$; Co) 15%, $\frac{3}{20}$; S) 20%, $\frac{1}{5}$

Grade 7 sectors: D) 72, 20%; Ca) 90, 25%; M) 54, 15%; Co) 108, 30%; S) 36, 10%

Grade 8 sectors: D) 72, $\frac{3}{10}$; Ca) 30, $\frac{1}{8}$; M) 42, $\frac{7}{40}$; Co) 84, $\frac{7}{20}$; S) 12, $\frac{1}{20}$

c. 237; $\frac{237}{900}$, or $\frac{79}{300}$; $26\frac{1}{3}$%

d. Tables may vary. Sample:

Gr	D	CA	MN	Co	Sn
6	30	105	60	45	60
7	72	90	54	108	36
8	72	30	42	84	12
St. Total	174	225	156	237	108
Fractions	$\frac{174}{900}$	$\frac{225}{900}$	$\frac{156}{900}$	$\frac{237}{900}$	$\frac{108}{900}$
Percents	$19\frac{1}{3}$%	25%	$17\frac{1}{3}$%	$26\frac{1}{3}$%	12%

Extension

Have students devise a survey and use it to collect data about the type of after-school events favored by students in your school. Students should organize their data and compare it to the Midfield Middle School data. Have them propose reasons for any significant differences between the sets of data.

Evaluation

Level	Standard to be achieved for performance at specified level
5	The student demonstrates a clear understanding of the relationships among fractions, decimals, and percents, and all calculations are accurate and complete. The student interprets the data reasonably and makes at least three sound observations regarding trends in data. The graph and the report are neat, thorough, and easy to read.
4	The student demonstrates a clear understanding of the relationships among fractions, decimals, and percents, but may make minor errors in calculations. The student interprets the data reasonably and makes several sound observations. The graphs and the report are neat and easy to read, but they may lack some detail.
3	There is a fundamental understanding of the relationships among fractions, decimals, and percents, but there may be one or more major errors or omissions in the student's work. The student is able to make an appropriate choice for labeling the graphs and can identify one or two trends in the data, but may need assistance getting started. The graphs and the report may contain significant errors.
2	The student demonstrates some understanding of the relationships among fractions, decimals, and percents, but is only able to convert among and operate with them with a great deal of assistance. The student is able to make an appropriate choice for labeling the graphs and can identify one or two trends in the data, but may need considerable prompting throughout the process. The student prepares the graphs and a report, but they are disorganized, inaccurate, and incomplete.
1	The student displays little understanding of fractions, decimals, percents, and the relationships among them. The student may attempt some calculations, but they are inappropriate and incorrect. There is no evidence that the student understands the given data, and there is no meaningful attempt to adjust the graphs or identify trends. Attempts at communication are jumbled and irrelevant.

Name _____

Chapter 4 Test Form C   Evaluation Guide

1. Complete this statement so that *both* the statement *and* its converse are true. Give the converse statement.

   If a number is odd, then

   _____.

   Complete the statement so that the statement is true, but its converse is false. Give the converse statement.

   If a number is odd, then

   _____.

Objectives E, H
- Writes statements that fit the criteria in the problem. Sample answers: it is 1 more than an even number; it is an integer
- Demonstrates understanding of the meaning of *converse*.
- Is able to write the converse of each if-then statement.

2. Give two inequalities so that the *intersection* of their solution sets on the number line is
   a. a point _____
   c. a segment _____
   b. a ray _____
   d. the empty set

   _____

   Give two inequalities so that the *union* of their solution sets on the number line is
   e. a line _____
   f. a ray _____

Objectives A, B, J
- Demonstrates understanding of *intersection* and *union*.
- Demonstrates understanding of *empty set*.
- Understands the concepts of point, segment, ray, and line.
- Is able to give inequalities that meet the given criteria.

3. Connect the points on the left to form a polygon. Name the polygon, and classify it according to the number of sides it has.

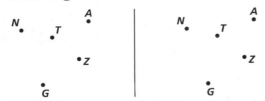

   Connect points on the right to form a figure that is not a polygon. Explain why the figure does not fit the definition of *polygon*.

Objectives B, F
- Demonstrates understanding of the definition of *polygon*.
- Correctly draws a polygon and a non-polygon.
- Identifies the polygon as a pentagon.
- Gives a correct name for the polygon.
- Correctly explains why the second figure is not a polygon.

4. This hierarchy shows some items sold in a clothing store. Make a hierarchy for a different type of store (for example, sporting goods, music, grocery, furniture). Your hierarchy should have at least six terms and at least three levels.

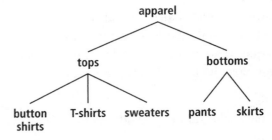

Objectives I, K
- Demonstrates understanding of a *hierarchy*.
- Hierarchy has at least six terms and three levels.
- Hierarchy correctly describes the relationships among the terms.

Chapter 4 Test Form D Evaluation Guide

Teacher Notes

Objectives B, C, E, G

Concepts and Skills This activity requires students to:

- know the properties of different types of quadrilaterals.
- recognize that there may be more than one correct definition for a term.
- rewrite a definition as an if-then statement and its converse.
- use drawings and logical reasoning to provide evidence that a statement is true.

Guiding Questions

- The if part of the statement will be of the form "If *something* is 'blank'" or "If *something* has 'blank'," What is the "something" in this case? What goes in the blank? What should the then part of the statement be?
- How could you use drawings to give evidence the statement is true? Is one drawing enough? What should be the same about the drawings? What could be different?

Answers

Students' statements should be close to the samples below. Check students' explanations and drawings.

Parallelogram:
If a quadrilateral has diagonals that divide each other in half, then it is a parallelogram.
If a quadrilateral is a parallelogram, then its diagonals divide each other in half.

Rectangle:
If a parallelogram has a right angle, then it is a rectangle.
If a parallelogram is a rectangle, then it has a right angle.

Rhombus:
If a parallelogram has two adjacent sides of the same length, then it is a rhombus.

Evaluation

Level	Standard to be achieved for performance at specified level
5	Student writes two correct if-then statements for all four quadrilaterals. For each of the eight statements, student presents neat, clear, and convincing evidence that the statement seems to be true.
4	Student writes two correct if-then statements for three quadrilaterals. For each of the six statements, student presents neat, clear, and convincing evidence that the statement seems to be true.
3	Student attempts to write if-then statements for three quadrilaterals. One or two of the six statements include errors. For each of the six statements, student presents evidence that the statement seems to be true. Some of the explanations may be incomplete or somewhat unclear.
2	Student writes only three or four correct statements. The others are not attempted or include significant errors. Students makes some attempt to provide evidence for the statements, but many of the explanations and drawings are incomplete, unclear, or illogical
1	Student attempts to write at least two or three of the if-then statements, but the statements include significant errors. Some attempt is made at providing evidence for the statements, but explanations show little evidence that student understands the task.

If a parallelogram is a rhombus, then it has two adjacent sides of the same length.

Square:
If a rhombus has diagonals of the same length, then it is a square.
If a rhombus is a square, then it has diagonals of the same length.

Extension

Have students try writing their own alternative definitions for one or more of the quadrilaterals. For example, a parallelogram may be defined as a quadrilateral with opposite sides that are the same length. A rhombus can be defined as a parallelogram with perpendicular diagonals.

Chapter 5 Test Form C Evaluation Guide

1. See page 62.

Objectives D, J
- Demonstrates an understanding of the triangle inequality.
- Gives the inequality $4 < x < 18$ for the possible lengths of the third side.
- Correctly constructs a triangle with the appropriate side lengths.

2. See page 62.

Objectives A, M
- Understands addition of positive and negative numbers.
- Is able to picture addition of positive and negative numbers.
- Recognizes that $-5 + 7 = 2$ and $5 + -7 = -2$.
- Draws an appropriate picture.

3. See page 62.

Objectives A, E
- Can add positive and negative numbers.
- Applies properties of addition to simplify expressions.
- Names three appropriate additions. Sample answers:
  a. $\frac{1}{4} + \frac{1}{3} + \frac{1}{12} = \frac{2}{3}$
  b. $-\frac{1}{3} + \frac{1}{3} + -\frac{5}{12} = -\frac{5}{12}$
  c. $\frac{3}{4} + -\frac{5}{12} + -\frac{1}{3} = 0$

4. See page 62.

Objectives C, I
- Understands the Take-Away, Comparison, or Slide Model of subtraction.
- Can solve an equation of the form $x - a = b$.
- Writes an appropriate problem. Sample problem: The temperature fell 5° between midnight and 6 A.M. At 6 A.M., the temperature was $-2°$. What was the temperature at midnight?
- Shows a correct solution and arrives at the answer 3.

5. See page 62.

Objectives H, N
- Understands the relationship between the probability of an event and the probability of its complement.
- Writes one of the following equations: $x + y = 1$, $x = 1 - y$, or $y = 1 - x$.
- Correctly graphs the equation, showing only points with coordinates greater than or equal to 0.

6. See page 62.

Objectives A, B, L
- Demonstrates understanding of absolute value.
- Demonstrates understanding of measures and magnitudes of rotations.
- Correctly states that a quarter rotation clockwise and a quarter rotation counterclockwise have measures that satisfy $|m| = 90°$.
- Describes three pairs of rotations that satisfy the equation. Sample answer: A half rotation clockwise, followed by a quarter rotation counterclockwise. Two rotations of 45° clockwise. A 60° counterclockwise rotation followed by a 30° counterclockwise rotation.

Chapter 5 Test Form D   Evaluation Guide

Teacher Notes

Objectives A, E, G, L

Concepts and Skills This activity requires students to:

- read information from text, a table, and a picture.
- make decisions based on given data and real-life experiences.
- add fractions and mixed numbers.
- calculate absolute value.
- Use the Putting-Together Model for Addition to form sentences involving addition.
- calculate magnitudes of turns.
- summarize results.

Materials

- rulers marked in customary units

Guiding Questions

- Why do you think the dashed-line path stops a few inches in front of the refrigerator?
- Why is the robot programmed to TURN 45 when it reaches the refrigerator?

Answers

a. Sample answer:
Trip to sink: TURN 45 MOVE $2\frac{1}{16}$ TURN −90 MOVE $3\frac{5}{8}$ TURN −90 MOVE $\frac{3}{4}$
Return trip: TURN 180 MOVE $\frac{3}{4}$ TURN 90 MOVE $3\frac{5}{8}$ TURN 90 MOVE $2\frac{1}{16}$ TURN 135

b. Sample answer: $12\frac{7}{8}$ yards

c. Answers will vary.

Extension

Have students identify paths between key points in the classroom, measure the distances, and create sets of commands to move the robot between the points.

Evaluation

Level	Standard to be achieved for performance at specified level
5	The student demonstrates an in-depth understanding of addition and measurement, and may ask several probing questions. All measurements and calculations are accurate and complete. The student may take the initiative to identify one or more alternative paths for any given location. The written report is neat, thorough, and easy to read, and it may be presented imaginatively.
4	The student demonstrates a clear understanding of addition and measurement. The student chooses several appropriate locations and paths for the robot, makes all necessary measurements, and performs all required calculations, but the work may contain minor errors. The written report is neat, thorough, and easy to read, but reflects the minor errors.
3	The student demonstrates a fundamental understanding of addition and measurement, but may need assistance in approaching the given situation. The student chooses several appropriate locations and paths for the robot, but there may be one or more major errors or omissions in the student's measurements and calculations. The report reflects these errors, and it may be somewhat disorganized and difficult to read.
2	The student demonstrates some understanding of addition and measurement. However, even with assistance, the student has a great deal of difficulty in choosing appropriate locations and paths for the robot. The student attempts to take measurements and calculate angles and distances, but there are significant errors or omissions. The student's report is jumbled and incomplete.
1	The student demonstrates little if any understanding of addition and measurement. Even when prompted, the student is unable to choose appropriate locations or paths for the robot. The student may take some measurements or perform some calculations, but they are superfluous or irrelevant. In preparing a written report, the student may simply copy or restate the given information.

Chapter 6 Test Form C Evaluation Guide

1. See page 79.

Objectives A, E
- Is able to draw the reflection image of a figure over a line.
- Can identify the symmetry lines of the figure.
- Completes the figure correctly, as shown below.
- Draws four lines of symmetry in the completed figure.

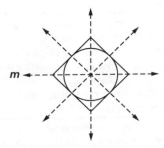

2. See page 79.

Objectives D, F, H
- Is able to find measures of angles in figures involving linear pairs, vertical angles, and perpendicular lines.
- Demonstrates the ability to find measures of angles in figures involving parallel lines and transversals.
- Writes 10 valid facts. Sample facts:
  $j \parallel k$; $n \perp k$; $m\angle 1 = m\angle 2 = m\angle 3 = m\angle 4 = m\angle 5 = 90°$; $m\angle 11 + m\angle 12 = 180°$; $m\angle 6 + m\angle 7 = 90°$; $m\angle 7 = m\angle 10$; $m\angle 7 = m\angle 12$; $m\angle 4 + m\angle 6 + m\angle 10 = 180°$; $m\angle 12 + m\angle 13 = 180°$; $m\angle 5 + m\angle 6 = m\angle 13$

3. Suppose your friend draws parallelogram *CPTQ* but does not show it to you. He tells you that $m\angle C = 65°$, $TQ = 3$ cm, and another side has length 5 cm. Do you have enough information to reproduce his parallelogram? If so, draw it and label all the side lengths and angle measures. If not, explain what additional information you need.

Objective G
- Understands the relationships among the sides and angles of a parallelogram.
- Recognizes that enough information is given.
- Draws and labels parallelogram *CPTQ*.

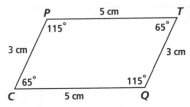

4. See page 79.

Objectives B, E
- Understands how to reflect and rotate figures.
- Correctly draws the reflection and rotation images:

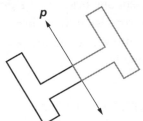

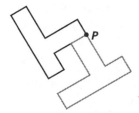

- Recognizes that the combination of the figure and its reflection image does have reflection symmetry.
- Recognizes that the combination of the figure and its rotation image does *not* have rotation symmetry.
- Provides a clear, correct explanation.

Chapter 6 Test Form D   Evaluation Guide

Teacher Notes

Objectives A, B, C, E

Concepts and Skills This activity requires students to:
- use data from text and pictures.
- make decisions based on given data and real life experiences.
- identify the symmetry lines of a figure.
- identify translations.
- apply the relationships between figures and their reflection and translation images.
- extend the fundamental region of a tessellation to cover a given area.
- find a percent of a number.
- estimate and calculate measurements and costs.
- summarize results.

Materials
- rulers
- graph paper

Guiding Questions
- How will you represent one brick on the graph paper? How will you represent the floor?
- Is there more than one way to estimate the number of bricks needed?

Answers
a. Jack-on-Jack (2 lines), Ladder Weave (1 line), Basket Weave Variation (2 lines)
b. Jack-on-Jack (2-fold), Traditional (2-fold), Whorling Square (4-fold), Basket Weave Variation (2-fold)
c. Herringbone
d. Whorling Square. Not all shapes in the pattern are congruent.
e. Answers will vary.
f. Answers will vary, but should be near 160.
e. Answers will vary, but should be near $220.

Extensions
Some paving bricks are made in the shape shown at the right. Have students determine

Evaluation

Level	Standard to be achieved for performance at specified level
5	The student demonstrates an in-depth understanding of transformations and tessellations and may offer additional insights or ask probing questions. All calculations are accurate and complete, and estimates are reasonable. The student's drawing is neat, thorough, and accurate, and it may be rendered imaginatively. The student may prepare two or more alternative patterns.
4	The student demonstrates a clear understanding of transformations and tessellations. The student plans an attractive pattern for the floor and prepares a drawing that is neat and easy to read, though it may lack in some detail. The student may make some minor errors in calculation or estimation, and these are reflected in the drawing.
3	The student demonstrates a fundamental understanding of transformations and tessellations. The student chooses a pattern and prepares a drawing that contains the essential elements of the pattern, but it may be somewhat disorganized and difficult to read. There may be one or more major errors or omissions in the student's calculations and estimates, and these are reflected in the drawing.
2	The student demonstrates some understanding of transformations and tessellations, but needs considerable help in applying the concepts to the given situation. There is an attempt to calculate the number of bricks and to estimate a cost, but the student makes one or more major errors or omissions in the process. The student's drawing is jumbled and incomplete.
1	The student demonstrates little if any understanding of transformations and tessellations. Even with prompting, the student is unable to choose a pattern or attempt the task of paving the floor. Any calculations or estimates are superfluous or irrelevant. The student may prepare a drawing by simply copying the given figures at random.

how the shape was created. Then have them use the basic 4-inch-by-8-inch rectangular shape to create their own original designs for paving bricks.

Assessing the Chapter Objectives

Chapter 1 SPUR Objectives	Chapter Test		
	Forms A and B	**Form C**	**Form D**
Skills			
A Perform arithmetic operations.	**9, 18**	**5**	
B Convert powers and word names for numbers to decimals.	**14**	**2, 5**	
C Use grouping symbols and the rules for the order of operations to evaluate numerical expressions.	**1–3**	**3**	
D Multiply by powers of ten.	**8, 17**	**2, 5**	
E Write numbers in scientific notation.	**6**	**2**	
Properties			
F Use < and > symbols to compare or order numbers.	**4, 20**	**4**	
G Know the definition of a rational number.	**12**	**1**	
H Recognize whether numbers are written in scientific notation.	**7**	**2**	
Uses			
I Interpret situations with two directions as positive, negative, or zero.	**19**	**4**	
J Understand uses of rational numbers in real situations.	**15, 16**	**1, 3**	
K Interpret information from scatterplots.	**10, 11**		√
Representations			
L Graph and read numbers on a number line.	**5**	**4**	
M Know the structure of the coordinate grid and how to represent data on it.	**13**	**6**	

Chapter 2 SPUR Objectives	Chapter Test		
	Forms A and B	**Form C**	**Form D**
Skills			
A Evaluate algebraic expressions given the values of all variables in them.	**2, 3, 14**	1	√
B Find solutions to equations and inequalities involving simple arithmetic.	**1, 13, 19**	1	√
C Write a numerical or algebraic expression for an English expression involving arithmetic operations.	**8**		
Properties			
D Find the length of the hypotenuse of a right triangle using the Pythagorean Theorem.	**17, 18**	3	
E Given instances of a pattern, write a description of the pattern using variables.	**9**	5	√
F Give instances of a pattern described with variables.	**7**		
Uses			
G Given instances of a real-world pattern, write a description of the pattern using variables.	**6**	4, 5	√
H Calculate the value of a variable given the values of other variables in a formula.	**16**		√
I Use the Pythagorean Theorem to find distances in real situations.	**15**	3	
Representations			
J Graph solutions to simple inequalities.	**10, 11**	2	
K Use a calculator or spreadsheet to construct formulas and apply them to real-life situations.	**12**		
L Represent a relationship between two variables using a table.	**4, 5, 20**	4	

Chapter 3 SPUR Objectives	Chapter Test		
	Forms A and B	**Form C**	**Form D**
Skills			
A Order and compare decimals and fractions.	**1, 8**	**1, 6**	√
B Add and subtract fractions.	**4, 7a, 22**	**2**	
C Round any number up, down, or to the nearest value of a fractional or decimal place.	**2**	**3**	
D Convert among decimals, fractions, and percents.	**3, 5, 6, 7b, 10, 11**	**4**	√
E Calculate the percent of a quantity.	**15**	**5**	√
F Estimate the square root of a number to a stated decimal place.	**16**		
Properties			
G Use the Equal-Fractions Property to rewrite fractions.	**14, 17**	**2**	√
H Correctly use the raised-bar symbol for repeating decimals.	**7c, 18**	**1**	
I Know and apply the Substitution Principle.	**19**	**4**	
Uses			
J Use fractions to answer questions in real situations.		**2**	
K Deal with estimates in real situations.	**12**	**3**	
L Use square roots in real situations.	**20b**	**6**	
M Calculate probabilities involving mutually exclusive events.	**13, 21**	**6**	
Representations			
N Graph and read numbers on number lines and coordinate grids.	**9**		
O Apply the geometric definition of a square root.	**20a**	**6**	

Chapter 4 SPUR Objectives	Chapter Test		
	Forms A and B	Form C	Form D
Skills			
A Determine the union and intersection of sets.	7	2	
B Draw and identify basic figures of geometry and polygons.	15, 23	2, 3	√
Properties			
C Identify statements as *always, sometimes but not always,* or *never* true.	3–6, 8, 9		√
D Apply the following properties: Additive Identity Property of Zero, Property of Opposites, and Opposite of Opposites Property.	1, 2		
E Write if-then statements and their converses.	10, 19, 24	1	√
F Apply the definition of polygon to various figures.	17	3	
G Apply the properties of a good definition.	11		√
H Identify the following types of numbers by their characteristics: real numbers, rational numbers, irrational numbers, positive numbers, negative numbers, integers, whole numbers, odd numbers, even numbers, and prime numbers.	16	1	
Uses			
I Apply hierarchies and Venn diagrams to real-world situations.	20, 21	4	
Representations			
J Describe unions and intersections of inequalities geometrically.	12–14	2	
K Use Venn diagrams and hierarchies to describe relationships among sets.	18, 22	4	

Chapter 5 SPUR Objectives	Chapter Test		
	Forms A and B	Form C	Form D
Skills			
A Add and subtract positive and negative numbers.	1, 2	2, 3, 6	√
B Calculate the absolute value.	3	6	
C Solve equations in the form $x + a < b$.	9, 17	4	
D Construct triangles using a compass and a straightedge.	12	1	
Properties			
E Apply properties of addition and subtraction to simplify expressions.	13	3	√
F Recognize uses of the Commutative and Associative Properties of Addition and the Addition Property of Equality.	14		
Uses			
G Use the Putting-Together and Slide Models for Addition to describe situations leading to addition.	6, 8		√
H Calculate probabilities involving mutually exclusive events or events with overlap.	4, 5	5	
I Use the Take-Away and Comparison Models for Subtraction to describe situations leading to subtraction.	18	4	
J Use the Triangle Inequality to approximate lengths of the third side of a triangle given the lengths of the other two sides.	19, 20	1	
Representations			
K Use fact triangles to depict relationships between numbers.	15, 16		
L Calculate magnitudes of turns given angle measures or revolutions.	10	6	√
M Graph addition and subtraction of positive and negative numbers using arrows on a number line.	11	2	
N Graph solutions to equations in the form $x + y = k$ or $x - y = k$.	7	5	

Chapter 6 SPUR Objectives	Chapter Test		
	Forms A and B	Form C	Form D
Skills			
A Reflect figures over a line.	1, 16	1	√
B Draw the rotation image of a point or figure.	10	4	√
C Create tessellations of polygons.	2, 18		√
D Use the Triangle-Sum Property to find measures of angles.	11	2	
Properties			
E Determine reflection and rotation symmetries of a figure.	12, 17	1, 4	√
F Use properties of lines and angles to determine angle measures.	4, 5, 19	2	
G Understand and use properties of parallelograms.	3, 14, 15	3	
H Explain consequences of the Triangle-Sum Property.	6, 20	2	
Uses			
I Use angle properties in everyday situations.	13		
Representations			
J Translate and reflect figures on a coordinate grid.	7, 8		
K Calculate the distance between two points on the coordinate plane.	9		